Plays, Players and Playing

How to Start Your Own Children's Theater Company

Judith A. Hackbarth

PICCADILLY BOOKS
COLORADO SPRINGS, COLORADO

Cover design by Michael Donahue

**Piccadilly Books
P.O. Box 25203
Colorado Springs, CO 80936
USA**

International sales and inquires contact:
  EPS
  20 Park Drive
  Romford Essex RM1 4LH, UK
or
  EPS
  P.O. Box 1344
  Studio City, CA 91614, USA

Library of Congress Cataloging-in-Publication Data
Hackbarth, Judith A.
    Plays, players and playing: how to start your own children's theater company / Judith A. Hackbarth.
        p.   cm.
    Includes bibliographical references and index.
    ISBN 0-941599-29-9
    1. Children's plays--Presentation, etc.   2. Theater--Production and direction.   3. Acting--Study and teaching.   I. Title.
PN3157.H28 1994
792'.0226--dc20   94-18425

Simultaneously published in Australia, UK, and USA
Printed in the United States of America

TABLE OF CONTENTS

INTRODUCTION

In the summer of 1981 I taught my first creative dramatics class. At that time I was a junior high English teacher. Although I didn't have a background in theater, I had been drafted during the school year to direct several school productions. Directing came easy to me and I enjoyed working with children outside of the classroom.

Like most teachers my income was limited, and I was constantly searching for ways to bring in more money. Teaching summer school was something I didn't particularly enjoy. Most of the kids dreaded being in school and the work generally centered around teaching remedial skills. I wanted to do something different! I also wanted a break from the rigid structure of a school classroom. For a short time, at least for the summer months, I wanted to be my own boss. I also wanted to teach. What kind of teachers are their own bosses? Individual tutors? That wasn't what I wanted. I had had enough of trying to get the basics across during the school year. I knew I wanted something more creative.

At that time, our community abounded in dance teachers. They certainly were creative and they were their own bosses. However, my dance skills were nonexistent, so that was out. Gymnastics? Another lucrative field. I couldn't even do a somersault! Theater? That was certainly more in my area; however, I'd never heard of an independent theater teacher except maybe in New York or Hollywood. I lived in a small rural Wisconsin town that didn't even have a decent movie theater. Who in the world would pay money for their child to take acting classes in New Richmond, Wisconsin, population somewhere around six thousand? Fortunately, I didn't take time to think about the probabilities; instead I placed an ad in the local paper and waited!

Eleven children enrolled. Enough, just barely, to stage a dazzling production of *Snow White*. That summer experience has evolved into a profitable and very enjoyable business! Today I own my own children's theater company and teach creative dramatics on a full-time basis!

Anyone who has an interest and talent in working with both theater and children can create a successful independent children's theater company. The term *successful* here meaning a company that can become a source of full-time income for not only the director but several other employees as well.

Dance teachers have been earning independent incomes for decades teaching the basics of ballet, tap, and jazz dancing to children in every corner of the United States. In the mid-seventies gymnastics teachers joined the ranks of independent business people and gymnastics studios sprang up across the country. Taking lessons has become the thing to do for the American child. There are independent business people everywhere offering lessons on everything from piano to karate. Why is it then that outside of the major cities like Los Angeles and New York acting studios for children are almost nonexistent?

One of the major problems is a lack of suitable facilities. A dance teacher can teach classes in any large room. Yearly recitals for dance can be staged in almost any facility that can seat an audience—from school gymnasiums to community civic centers. Dancers rarely need special lighting or sound effects or even a curtain before they are ready to stage a performance. When gymnastics became the rage several years ago, teachers rarely had difficulty finding a facility. Gymnastics calls for large equipment, but all of it can be assembled and disassembled quite quickly, so gymnasts could easily share any large open area with others.

Acting is not as simple. While acting classes and even

rehearsals for productions can be held in a large classroom, the actual production of a play needs to be staged in a performing complex of some kind. Scenery constructed for a play cannot be easily set up and taken down. To stage a play effectively, the sound in a room needs to be easily heard. There should be some kind of a lighting system available, and there needs to be room backstage so that actors can make entrances and exits easily.

Another problem with viewing acting in the same business category as dance and gymnastics is that children generally are exposed to the dramatic arts in some form everyday whereas dance and gymnastics appear to be more specialized areas. A child does not receive dance classes in school except maybe the once a year effort by a physical education teacher. Therefore, a parent who wants their child exposed to dance must pay for the privilege. Gymnastics is offered in educational programs but only on a limited basis. Once again, parents must pay for the opportunity if they want their child to receive more training. The same is true for piano, karate, and any other art or sport that is not sanctioned by the educational system.

The opportunity for children to act, however, surrounds them daily. Teachers and child-care workers are constantly putting on plays. A child may play an angel in the annual church Christmas pageant or an Indian in the yearly cub scout roundup-day celebration. They may put on a play in their school or perform a skit with the local 4-H club. The opportunities for children to be on stage are endless. So, why should parents enroll their child in an independent acting company and even pay a tuition for an activity a child can easily pick up elsewhere?

To be successful, an independent acting teacher must establish that acting is as specialized an area as dance or gymnastics. While children may have the opportunity to participate in dramatic arts activities in school, few schools, if any, offer acting technique as part of their curriculum. Generally, when a school or other children's organization stages a play, they are doing it as a one-time special event. The amount of time spent rehearsing is minimal, and the children are expected to do no more than recite their lines word for word. Children dress in "cute" costumes, they make "cute" scenery, and overall everyone looks and acts "cute." Parents love seeing their own child on stage, but for nonparents these productions can be tedious and boring.

Becoming a member of a professional theater company allows children the opportunity to learn how to become characters that audiences outside of Mom and Dad will come to see. Learning the art of acting helps children develop self-confidence and assuredness that will stay with them the rest of their lives. In professional theater, a child is no longer "nine-year old Timmy from Mrs. Baxter's fourth-grade class" whom Mom and Dad came to see read the part of Tom Sawyer. Instead, in a professional theater company and in the accompanying classes and rehearsals, a child learns to convincingly become Tom Sawyer complete with Tom's mannerisms and personality. Together with the audience, Tom then sets out on a series of adventures which takes him and the audience out of a 20th century reality and into the Hannibal, Missouri, of the early 1800s.

The dictionary defines a professional as one who has an assured competence in a particular field. An acting teacher provides the company members with the competencies needed in theater so that they can eventually win the label of "professional" in the same way that a dance teacher helps a child learn competencies of dance and a gymnastics teacher guides a child toward the competencies needed to become a first-class gymnast. As in dance and gymnastics, acting competencies cannot be achieved over-night. They cannot be learned by a one-time appearance as a rabbit in the school Easter pageant. Acting skills need to be taught and nurtured, and a children's acting company is the place to start.

Finding success on the stage and winning the approval of the audience can be an exciting experience for children and can play an important part in their futures. Children who learn professional theater skills learn to have self-confidence in new situations, they learn to be comfortable with their own abilities, and they learn to trust their inner talents. And, when the audience applauds them for their acting skills, children learn that working hard and striving for excellence bring rewards.

THE COMPANY

GETTING STARTED

You enjoy working in theater. You enjoy working with children. It seems natural to put the two together. But where do you begin? How do you find children who have an interest in theater? Where do you find a facility to perform in? How do you raise the money for beginning expenses? What about costumes, props, scenery, lighting, tickets, programs, and scripts? These are all realistic questions to ask yourself when starting a children's theater company. However, the first question you should ask yourself is why?

WHY CHILDREN'S THEATER?

Do you want to see children involved in drama because it will be an educational experience, or are you simply looking for a quick tuition dollar? Do you want to organize a children's theater group to provide children in your community a chance for creative expression, or does it seem like an easy way to make some extra

The Stagedoor kids in *The Wizard of Oz.*

income? Extra income and a quick tuition dollar may sound enticing, but all of the dollars you receive for working in children's theater will be well earned. Money should not be your reason for working in children's theater.

However, if you have an interest in providing a valuable educational experience, children's theater can be your forte. Drama helps children understand that they are individuals with special abilities. It also helps them gain skills in a variety of different areas from acting to play writing to designing costumes and constructing scenery. Drama can help children improve their concentration, creativity, and self-confidence. It will help them learn to understand and accept other people and other people's beliefs, thoughts, and dreams.

In creative dramatics, children gain confidence in oral language and learn to express feelings and portray moods. The exciting experiences they have on stage, complete with the approval and applause from an eager audience, help to boost their perception of themselves.

For the community, a children's theater company can be called upon to provide entertainment at community festivals or special events. Civic groups can use a children's theater company as entertainment when planning community picnics or dinners. A children's theater company can help promote educational themes by presenting programs on drug addiction, child abuse, or local history. The community library can rely on a children's theater company to kick off special book celebrations such as Tom Sawyer days or Raggedy Ann and Andy week. For both adults and children in the community, children's theater offers a multitude of educational and entertainment ideas.

On the other hand, as a business enterprise, children's theater can be quite lucrative. Fees can be charged for classes and productions. Tickets can be sold for attendance to the performances. Children will be eager to purchase T-shirts, sweatshirts, and jackets imprinted with their acting company logo. Working with children, a director can develop scripts that can be sold to other theater groups or play publishing companies.

SETTING GOALS

No matter what your individual reason may be for wanting to start a children's theater company, getting it started can be challenging and you must have a clear cut goal in mind before you begin. Is your goal to operate this theater company as a hobby or as a career? Do you plan to be profit oriented or will you be organizing a nonprofit community theater?

Over 75 percent of the theaters in this country operate on a nonprofit basis. This means that they are organized by a group of people and decisions are made by a board of directors. The advantage of nonprofit theater is in the amount of funding and volunteer labor that you may be able to accumulate from other organizations. Often, large corporations or local arts organizations will help nonprofit theater organizations by donating money or materials to launch a production. No one will donate money to an individual wanting to start his or her own business.

A distinct disadvantage to becoming nonprofit relates to the organizing and teaching of acting classes which are the basis of a successful program. Most nonprofit theater groups can accumulate funding only for the actual productions they stage. The time you put into the planning and teaching of classes for a nonprofit organization will probably not be funded. This means that reimbursing you for your time while teaching classes may be difficult to do. Nonprofit organizations do not have the funding to pay individuals more than a minimal salary, and therefore they rely primarily on volunteer, nonprofessional labor. Teaching classes requires some degree of professionalism in the field.

However, deciding to operate a children's theater company on a for-profit level is a decision that should not be made lightly. Offering acting classes as a business encompasses the same conditions that dance and gymnastics teachers face. Few gymnastic or dance instructors teach regularly for nonprofit organizations. They are teaching classes for a career and need to make a reliable income from their classes. Most operate their own studios on a for-profit basis and charge considerable sums for their classes.

To operate your program as a business, you must charge enough of a tuition to cover your costs and the time you have invested. You must enroll in an insurance program to cover your liability costs in case a child is injured in one of your classes. You must be willing to keep your accounting books up to date, and you must be willing to assume total responsibility for the quality of your company's productions. Once you establish a reputation as a for-profit business, you cannot expect donations of costumes, props, or money. Nor will people be as willing to volunteer their time to help out.

A scene from *Tumbleweeds*.

On the more positive side, you will own your business and can make any decisions regarding it. You will not have to answer to a board of directors or worry about being fired. You can be assured that the quality of your productions will be consistent since you will be the one responsible for the outcome.

MAKING A COMMITMENT

Before you can make a decision on whether your theater company will be operated on a nonprofit or for-profit status, you must decide what the extent of your own personal commitment will be. Are you planning on being involved on a full-time basis? Will you be offering classes as well as directing plays? Or, do you just want to help start the group and then plan on limiting your involvement? No program can be successful without dedicated personnel committed to success. Working with children can be stressful, and the people who make a commitment to children's theater must really believe in the value of it.

Let us determine here and for the remainder of this book that you have decided to enter into operating a children's theater company on a full-time basis. You want to offer classes and stage productions on a regular basis, and you want to do it as a business and earn a respectable salary doing it. So how do you get started? What's the first step? First of all, take a quick inventory of your resources.

Do you have any contact with local schools? Do you personally know any teachers or administrators? These people will be your best source of potential students and troupe members. Get out into the community as much as possible and introduce yourself. Offer to teach a few free drama classes for the elementary school, volunteer your services to a 4-H club, or boy scout or girl scout troop. Get your face known among organizations that deal with children. They will be your best referral source.

Do you have any money for starting up this type of a business? You will probably need $3,000 to $5,000 to launch your business. You will need to purchase a minimal amount of supplies such as a tape recorder, tapes for movement and imagination exercises, crayons, paper, bookkeeping supplies, and classroom props, as well as pay for advertising fees and so forth. You will need money to pay the rent for rehearsal/classroom space. You will also need to purchase liability insurance on your space. If you cannot afford renting a space for your classes, you may want to work out an exchange with a local private school. They are generally eager to have specialists work in their building in exchange for services to their students. Offer to direct the annual school play in exchange for free rehearsal space all year. You may decide that you want to take out a small business loan to get you started. Ask your local banker to direct you in the area of obtaining special arts loans that are often available to new businesses.

Do you have the skills needed for set construction, costuming, and prop making? You may want to find a few reliable associates in your community. If you are to direct the play and teach classes, you will definitely need help in designing and building the set and making costumes and props. Try to obtain names of community people talented in this area, and then offer them a trade; perhaps they have a child that would benefit from your classes in exchange for their services.

Where will you hold your classes and perform productions? Take a walking tour of your community. In addition to the local schools, check out church basements, civic centers, and local libraries. All are potential meeting places for a drama group. Accept that an acting company does not need to meet in a performing complex in order to be successful. Theater can happen anywhere.

Do you know anything about advertising or promotional concepts? Getting the word out to your future members and audiences is vitally important. A theater company cannot be successful without an audience. If you do not have any knowledge on how to write an ad or draw up a poster, you may want to stop in and talk with an advertising specialist at your local newspaper. Ask for advice on how to reach potential customers. Most newspapers will be happy to help you in this area, providing you advertise with them.

Do you have a strong network of friends, relatives, or community members to back you? A theater company is generally a strong network of people. If you are going to be successful in this area, you will want to know that you are going to have help. Even if you are starting a for-profit business, you will find that there is enough interest in theater to bring in some volunteer help. Obviously, you will not be able to get as much volunteer labor as if it were a nonprofit venture, but everyone loves a play; and if you have a strong circle of friends, you should be able to draw them into the fun.

TROUPE MEMBERS

WHY CHILDREN ENJOY ACTING

Children enjoy acting because it helps them understand the confusion of the real world. In the fantasy world of make-believe, a child can experiment with roles and feelings that often cause them confusion. How does it feel to be the little clown that nobody wants to play with or the dragon who isn't brave? Why does everyone like the adventurous Tom Sawyer and despise his studious brother, Sid? Why does Peter Rabbit's mother punish him for just wanting to have fun? Why would Dorothy choose to go home when she could stay in Oz with her friends? Questions like these are answered in children's plays and help to make a child's understanding of the world a little easier.

Growing up in today's world can be difficult. A child has easy access to R-rated movies on television one night, and then the next night they hop into bed eagerly awaiting the tooth fairy. Their realities are constantly confused. On stage there is no reality. A child enters a world in which he or she does not have to understand anything. Alice falls down the rabbit hole because it is a make-believe story. Cinderella becomes a princess because it is a make-believe story. Peter Pan flies to Neverland because it is a make-believe story. In a world in which reality can be confusing and sometimes even dangerous, the make-believe arena of theater gives a child a sense of security.

Throughout their childhood years, children are searching for their identity. The theater gives children the opportunity to

Troupe members show off their T-shirts.

experiment with different identities.   Through the magic of the
stage, they can temporarily become the mischievous Puck in *A
Midsummer Night's Dream* or the impertinent Anne in *Anne of
Green Gables*. They can be as mean as the witch in *Snow White*
or as nice as Snow White herself. They can be old, young, or
ageless. They can be smart or dumb, adventurous or quiet.

Acting gives children confidence and poise. It helps children
develop skills in concentration, observation, and communication. It
helps them gain recognition among their peers. It helps them in
their difficult identity search by allowing them to try on different
personalities and choose the characteristics they most admire.
Becoming a member of an acting company can be an exciting and
educational experience.

WHO WILL BELONG TO THE TROUPE?

Will the children in your company come directly from your own community, or will they be commuting? How many children will be included in the initial company? How old will they be? Will the children all be from one specific age group, or will the company be a mixture of children of all ages? Are the children from a low-income area, or are they from a high-income area? What is the ethnic background of the majority of the children?

It is best, whenever possible, to combine age groups. Working with only one age group limits the choice of productions that can be staged. Also, younger children thrive on being around older ones. Remember, the younger children are the basis for a successful future. Seven is the earliest age that I would recommend becoming an official theater troupe member. Tot classes can be offered to younger children, but stage experience should wait until a child is at least seven. Children need to be old enough to understand their stage experience.

Choosing an ending or cut-off age for your troupe can also be difficult. Although the ending age in a children's theater group can be anywhere from fifteen to eighteen, it is good to avoid too many older children. Older children can overshadow the younger ones causing the younger ones to lose interest. Also, older children are more difficult to control and are involved in more extracurricular activities which may interfere with rehearsal time.

Choosing the right children to belong to a theater group can be a difficult task. Where do you find individuals that will be the most committed? All children enjoy performing and pretending, but not all children are willing to give up precious playtime for tedious rehearsal hours. It is important to the professionalism of the group that the children are selected according to their interest, not necessarily according to their talent. Children that are truly interested in being at rehearsals and attending classes will in the long run give the best performance. When children are really interested and want to be involved, they won't complain about rehearsal length, they won't refuse to memorize long sections of dialogue, and they won't try to cause mischief when they aren't on stage.

If children audition for membership in the company, it is important to audition their interest level in addition to their acting ability. Do they really want to be on stage? Do they mind giving up after-school television time to rehearse? Do they enjoy watching plays? Would they be happy with a small role, or do they only want to appear in plays in which they can have a big part? Sometimes a child may shine in an audition but is only there because mother insisted, and in reality the child has no desire to be on stage. A quieter child in the audition may have a burning desire to perform. This type of a child can be molded into a wonderful actor or actress. Always choose the children who want to be involved.

Children are natural performers and with a little training they can do wonderful things on stage. That's why interest level plays such an important part in finding potential people. When children are really interested in something, they embrace it to the fullest. Children don't just collect one baseball card, they fill albums with them. Children don't just color one picture in a coloring book. If they are interested in coloring, they will sit for hours and fill up the whole book. This kind of dedication and concentration can be found in children interested in acting. When they are really interested, they are willing to spend hours at rehearsal. They are willing to give up time for costume fittings. They don't mind performing during vacation times. Once children have decided to be interested in something, they will generally give it their all.

So, how do you find these dedicated souls? Start with a promotional campaign. Make becoming a member of your acting company sound exciting. Place ads, hand out flyers, talk to organizations where children congregate, and recruit interested children. Don't wait for them to come to you, go looking for troupe members.

FINDING A NAME

Choose a name for your acting group that tells your audiences that you are not just a children's social club performing for parents only. Instead, your title should indicate that you a serious company dedicated to the performing arts. This name also lets potential members know that you want only those children who are really interested in theater to join you.

It helps to have a logo of some kind designed right away. If you aren't artistic, have an artist help you put together something interesting. Something that says "We are . . ." to the public.

Taking the time to choose a name for your group and having a logo designed is a symbol of your faith that you will succeed. This lets everyone, both the public and the company members, identify that you are a professional group. As professionals, your sole purpose will be to present high-quality productions.

The logo for my acting company, which you see above, lets parents and kids know that I expect them to achieve star status in this group. The child on the logo also lets kids know that this will be a children's group. Once you have a design, take your logo and go to the local newspaper. Ask them to help you create a small ad that you can place in their paper. When the ad is ready, ask them to put it in the family section of the paper where parents are sure to see it.

You may also use this logo on a flyer that can be distributed to the elementary school students in your town. You can put up posters in fast food restaurants and toy stores. Let school administration, churches, and youth groups know that you will be starting a theater group exclusively for children.

INTERVIEWING POTENTIAL MEMBERS

When you have completed your promotional efforts, you should have some response. You may only have five children who show up for the first auditions, or you may get five hundred. Whatever the number, try to interview each child individually and find out why they want to act. If possible, have this interview in private or with someone other than a parent present. When the parents are around children tend to tell you what they think Mom or Dad want them to say. Ask a child individually, "Why are you here? What do you want to get out of acting?"

Your productions will be made up of many different personalities. Try to select a varied group of performers. You will need children of different ages and, of course, different sexes. If you can find children from varied ethnic backgrounds, it will give your company an added versatility. Children who have forceful voices and are willing to try any role are a valuable addition to any acting company, but so too are the soft-spoken children who are content with a minor part.

When you have selected your group, try to get to know the children before casting a play. This involves a few pre-show workshops in which you can determine the ability level of each child. It generally takes a director at least a year or so to determine the individual characteristics of individual actors. A student who can be a success as the mischievous Tom Sawyer might feel ridiculous as Raggedy Andy and thereby not perform to the peak of his ability. It is up to the director to get to know the children so that the casting of the play will highlight the actor's personality, not limit it.

When a cast looks as though they are having lots of fun on stage, the audience will just naturally join in the excitement. Choose company members that can radiate this kind of atmosphere. It is important and necessary to the success of your productions.

FACILITIES

You have your cast. Now what? Choosing a home base for your acting company can be almost as frustrating as finding troupe members.

During the first five years that I taught drama classes independently, I tried a variety of different facilities. Although I now own my own building, I started out renting space in the local civic center. It was a small rectangular room in the basement with barely enough room for my first eleven students and myself. From there I tried a racquet ball court during the time of the day when it wasn't usually scheduled. Next, I tried a community education meeting hall, an elementary school classroom, and a church's Sunday school room before finally settling in at the local Catholic elementary school.

By the time I settled at the Catholic school, I had left public school teaching to pursue a career in teaching drama full-time, so my funds were rather limited. I made a deal with the local Catholic elementary school. I would use their school gym immediately after school on Tuesdays and Thursdays in exchange for teaching a drama group for the school during the school day. There were advantages and disadvantages to doing this.

A performance in progress.

First of all, the principal hadn't mentioned that we might have to move occasionally to another room during the basketball season. The basketball season extends from mid-October until the first of March. That made for more than just an occasional move. Also, the echo in a gymnasium is terribly irritating when you are trying to teach such concepts as projection and tone. I found my head kept ringing for several hours after I finished teaching a class. Then, of course, there was the added factor of the children in my classes who enjoyed, just a little too much, having a gym to themselves. I found myself having to make several deals with them for shorter class times so that they would have time to shoot baskets before they went home.

The main advantage to being in the Catholic school, however, was that for the first time I had a space that was reliable and happy to have me. The school allowed me to store my costumes and props in their old convent rooms that were no longer being used. I was also allowed to leave my set pieces and flats on the stage in the gymnasium. In exchange for leaving my things at the school rent free, I allowed the school to use my materials whenever they wanted.

FINDING A PERFORMING SPACE

Finding a place to teach classes was much easier than finding a place to perform productions. Classes can basically take place anywhere, even in your own home, if you have the space. Productions, in which an audience will be present, must be performed in a space that is labeled safe by your local building inspector. You cannot cram audiences into a room that does not have enough exits. You cannot perform in a room that does not meet fire code regulations. You cannot block exits or extinguishers with flats or set pieces.

Independent rental property, although it may provide the space you need, probably won't meet the safety codes you will be facing when performing for an audience. Schools, churches, civic centers, and most public meeting places are designed to meet safety regulations for large groups. Naturally, an existing theater space, if it is available, may seem like the ideal situation, but that isn't always the case. Rental for such places can be extremely high, and often scheduling time in one is a major problem.

Until I purchased my own theater, I spent many frustrating summers performing in our local high school auditorium. There was no air-conditioning so it was always very hot. Plus, summertime is the school's cleaning time, and the theater was almost always the last priority on the custodian's busy schedule, so it was always dirty.

Children's theater, even in a public school auditorium, is given little priority, and so we always had to wait until the community scheduled their events before we could pick our performing dates. Then, we might unexpectedly have to rearrange if the theater was needed for a more important activity. One summer, the day before our performance of *Alice In Wonderland,* the annual community beauty queen talent contest decided to use the theater at the last minute. It meant that we had to strike our entire set and put it up again the next day.

During the winter time when the school facilities were booked with their own activities, I arranged to have my students perform at a local country club. This was generally a much better situation because we didn't have to share the facility with anyone. No one uses a country club in the winter. However, we did have to haul our materials out in the cold; and, on many sub-zero days, I found myself questioning why I had gotten myself into children's drama.

WHAT TO LOOK FOR IN A PERFORMING SPACE

Selecting a facility to house your acting company can sometimes seem like an impossible task. Accept first that an acting company does not need to meet in a performing complex in order to be successful. Theater can happen anywhere. Look for a facility that offers you the following:

Privacy
Children become distracted very easily, so you need a classroom or rehearsal hall which offers some privacy from other groups.

Acoustics
The room should be echo-free but large enough for movement activities. Gymnasiums and other high ceilinged rooms may seem ideal at first, but most have sound problems that can leave the director/teacher frustrated at the end of a session.

Storage
The more storage the better. Theater companies quickly accumulate costumes, props, and scenery that will have to be stored

somewhere. It is a definite advantage to the group to store it close
to the rehearsal area.

Easy Entrances
If the facility you choose is not located in a school, the parents will
have to deliver their children to and from classes and rehearsals.
Try to find a space that offers adequate parking and safety from
traffic hazards. If children will have to enter the building alone,
make sure that the hallways are safe and well-lighted. Never hold
classes or rehearsals involving children in areas that have potential
danger.

Performing Space
Ideally, you would want to find a space that can serve as both
rehearsal hall and stage area. This may be impossible since most
stages are booked by adult groups. Children's theater is often at the
bottom of the list in scheduling priority. Keep in mind that a
performing space need not include a formal stage but must meet
adequate safety requirements. Many successful off-broadway
groups perform in what are called black box theaters. These are
just large square rooms that can adequately hold an audience of
anywhere from fifty to two hundred people. Black box theaters
offer the director versatility in staging. This versatility combined
with children's natural creativity can provide an excellent change
from traditional theater.

Accessibility
This is not as important for your classes because the materials you
will use in teaching are generally quite portable and can be
transported in a box or basket. However, when you perform in a
complex that is not your own, you may need to transport scenery
and large props. You should check to see if there is an outside
stage door in which you can transfer items to the stage. Measure
entrances. You will meet with an endless amount of frustration if
your set pieces turn out to be just a little too big to fit through the
theater doors.

WHERE TO LOOK

Finding the best performing and teaching areas is an important step towards success. Take your time. Look over your choices carefully. Be innovative. Theater can happen anywhere and often the most successful theaters are the ones who dare to be different. When you begin to investigate within your community, you will probably find a number of places that will fit your needs. Here are a few suggestions of where to begin.

Schools
Talk to your local school superintendent and explain your ideas. You may be offered a classroom that is not in use which could become a permanent home for your troupe.

Park Districts
Many community park districts have clubhouses located in the bigger neighborhoods. Ask to tour one of these facilities. Often they are empty in the evening hours.

Churches
Most churches today have Sunday school rooms that are empty during the week. Talk to your local clergy and see if these rooms could be made available for rent. During the summer months, they may just lie empty all day.

Homes for the Elderly
Nursing homes are always looking for entertainment. They also enjoy having young people come into their facility. There may be a large cafeteria or visitor's lounge that could be made available for acting classes in exchange for residents peeking in during the sessions.

Hospitals

Hospitals often have large meeting rooms that are empty during the early evening hours. You may be able to rent space with an agreement to stage a short show for patients occasionally.

Libraries

Many community libraries have large meeting rooms that have been designed to handle community meetings. Talk to your local librarian and find out what the opportunities are for renting space.

Community Centers

A city hall usually has rooms that can be made available for community classes. Visit your local civic center and check it out.

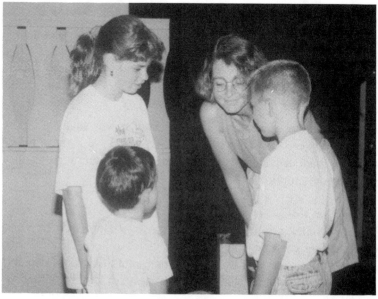

The director takes time to discuss a problem in the script.

Restaurants
Dinner theater is always a fun activity. Visit your local restaurants and see if they would be interested in sponsoring a production in return for allowing you to use their rooms for your classes.

Real Estate Agents
It never hurts to go to the experts. A real estate agent may know of a business or organization that has rooms to rent. Real estate agents can also help you connect with other independent teachers looking for space. Perhaps a local karate teacher or gymnastic instructor would like to share space.

THE DIRECTOR

Organizing a children's theater company demands a tremendous commitment and is a major responsibility. Without a doubt, the most important aspect of a children's theater group will be the director or leader. There must be one person who will be in charge. This may not be the person who teaches the classes or even directs the play. However, this will be the person who sets up the schedules, registers the actors and actresses, deals with the parents, handles the publicity, and overcomes the many problems that a children's theater group will encounter.

Working with children, no matter what subject area you choose, requires a great deal of patience. However, in addition to patience, the individual who leads a children's theater must have a tremendous amount of respect for children. Without that respect, it becomes virtually impossible to get children to dedicate themselves in a professional manner. The director or motivator of a children's theater group must believe unconditionally that children are just as capable as adults at turning out professional theater.

I have seen actors with a tremendous amount of experience in theater, either in college, community, or professional theater, who have failed horribly with a children's group. The success of a director in children's theater does not lie in how much education or personal experience one has encountered in the theater, but in how much time, effort, and commitment the individual is willing to give to the children's drama presentations and to the children themselves as individuals.

Unlike most university instructors, I believe that a degree in theater is not necessary to become a children's theater director. A degree in elementary education would be more appropriate along with an inborn dramatic talent. Children do not judge people by their degree. A master's degree or even a doctorate has little effect on a room full of eager eight-year olds. A smile, casual clothing, eagerness, and enthusiasm go much further with children. But obviously, children might not pick the most qualified adult to be their director if they had the ultimate choice. Therefore, who should be the director of a children's theater group?

QUALIFICATIONS OF A DIRECTOR

The director of children's theater must take the job seriously. Too many times directors of children's productions go about their jobs in a haphazard way. They acknowledge to themselves that directing any play is better than directing none; however, they secretly believe that children's theater isn't any more important than simply bringing a smile to the faces of the doting parents. This is the wrong sort of person to direct children's theater. An ideal director is someone with the following traits:

A Diehard
A person who has the ability to tackle the impossible and mold it into something probable.

A Dreamer
Someone who can see the potential in a shy personality and help it emerge into a blossoming talent.

An Organizer
The type of person who enjoys making lists, lists, and more lists and knows how to make sure the lists are completed.

An Authority Figure
Possibly a disciplinarian who can handle not only the stubborn child but also the stubborn parent.

A Reader
Someone who is willing to pore through volumes of poorly written plays for children until a suitable script for the troupe can be discovered.

An Achiever
A person who is not content to do a "cute" job but strives for professionalism in children's theater.

A Talker
Not only must this individual out-talk the children but also must out-talk everyone. This person must be able to reason with unreasonable parents, soothe egotistical board members, calm irate ticket buyers, compliment sensitive technical directors, and encourage fragile child egos.

A Writer
Someone who can take a script and rewrite it for individual personalities in order to achieve optimum results.

A Futurist
Someone who refuses to let up when the going gets rough. Someone who will not listen to the whining and complaining, but hears only the needs of the group and looks forward to the future.

INTERVIEWING A POTENTIAL DIRECTOR

When interviewing a potential director, or if you are trying to determine if you yourself could direct a children's theater presentation, ask the following questions:

Do you really enjoy being around children, lots of them, constantly?

A children's theater director, once the play is into rehearsal, spends much of the day with children and the rest of the time thinking about them.

Can you handle the constant fighting and horseplay involved in children's theater?

Keep in mind that kids will be kids. This is a fact that I would hope the potential director can not only handle but heartily approve. Kids fight, they scream, they tease, they are mean, they are loving. Every emotion that adults try so hard to hide comes right to the surface with children.

Do you view children as individuals with individual talent?

In casting a children's production, it is vitally important for the director to be able to see below the surface. Children can be shy at times, especially around their peers. It is up to the director to be aware of even the slightest potential and help to bring it to the surface.

Do you respect the questions, fears, and concerns that the parents have concerning their child's involvement?

The classic stage mother still lives. I have no doubts about that. Fortunately, most directors in community theater or school groups will not have to contend with this type of individual. However, many of the questions parents pose to directors concerning their child's performance still have very little to do with the total performance and more to do with the individual child's needs. "Could you see that Johnny doesn't talk too much today—he has a sore throat?" "Does Sarah have to be at rehearsal tomorrow—she has a make-up piano lesson?" A children's theater director needs to realize that a child cannot be completely responsible for getting to and from rehearsals by themselves. They are dependent on their parents, and their parents' schedules come first. Understanding this factor will help to relieve a lot of the stress children's theater directors face on a daily basis.

Can you handle tackling a job with very little to no recognition?

As a director of children's theater for the past fifteen years, I have still not received acknowledgement for being a "real" director. Invariably the comments will be made by some kindly old matron who has directed high school drama for years that the person over there, meaning me, directs some really cute children's stories. Unfortunately, too many people view children's theater as a play activity rather than as a dramatic art form.

Do you have an overactive imagination?

A director of children's theater must accept whenever possible, such theories as blue is pink, green is red, this box is a horse, that wall is a castle and so on. Without this imaginative ability, the director will not be able to offer the world of fantasy to either the actors or audience.

If your potential director has managed to answer most of these questions and still sits before you with a grin, you've probably found the right person. If instead, your potential candidate was yawning or gritting his teeth at the questions, simple as they were, you probably should consider someone else. It is likely that this type of person looks down on children's plays. At this point if you would just casually mention that you are also in need of a director for the adult theater group's presentation of *Hamlet* and he drops to his knees and begs for the position, you know you have the wrong person. An individual who would rather direct *Hamlet* than *Little Red Riding Hood* is not who you want, look further.

PARENTAL INVOLVEMENT

Anyone who works with children will also have to learn to work with parents. Children's personalities vary from the responsible, easy to direct child to the always late, never has his lines learned child. The personalities of the parents vary as well. You will encounter the typical stage mom who wants her child to be the star of every production whether the child can act or not. Then, too, you will meet parents who very rarely show their faces except at occasional performances. Hopefully, you will find parents who are between these two extremes and are always supportive of their children but allow them to find their own niche in life. These are the parents you want to work with, and the parents you will need to help build a successful program.

A director of children's theater must learn to work with parents as allies. You must learn to be courteous and patient with even the most obnoxious, pushy parents. Channeled into the right direction, even difficult parents can be helpful when it comes to staging a production. Generally, I've found that the parents who push their children hard to achieve are really just trying to fill a gap in their own lives. Get this type of parent involved.

One mother I dealt with was always quite upset when her daughter didn't get a big part. The child on the other hand preferred to play the smaller parts. She didn't want the responsibility or the attention that the larger roles commanded. But she did want to make her mother happy. The mother continued to be

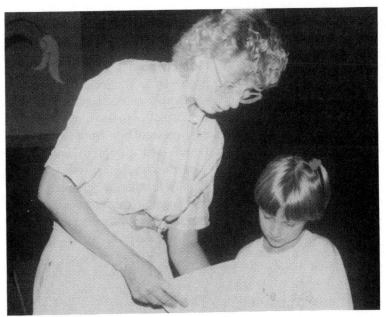

Parents can help their children memorize lines.

difficult despite her daughter's wishes until I asked her to handle
publicity for one of our productions. That was all it took! The
mom enjoyed being in the limelight with our advertisers. She took
it upon herself to set up radio interviews and special newspaper
articles. She even convinced several nursery schools to attend our
production. She channeled all the energy she usually put forth
controlling her child into the publicity for our show. She was so
busy that she didn't have time to think about what part her
daughter had received. The daughter relaxed without the added
pressure from her mother and took a very small role and turned it
into a scene stealer. The mom forgot to count how many lines her
child had in the play. When she finally saw her daughter on stage,
she was impressed with the "big" role she had.

Most parents are eager to get involved in their children's activities. However, they are hesitant to do so because they don't want to embarrass their child. This is a valid concern. Kids need to be independent. They don't want or need their parents hovering over them before they go on stage. Once at a local dance recital, I walked backstage to give a mother a message, and I was surprised to see the number of mothers primping their daughters before they went on. These children were not being taught to be responsible. They could rely on their parent to know what costumes they needed and when their entrances were. This is robbing children of a very important learning experience.

When children are in charge of their own costumes, props, entrances, and exits, they learn to be responsible. I generally have one parent backstage and that is only to maintain a quiet set. One thing that children have a hard time mastering when they are in a group is how to be quiet. The presence of an adult can make all the difference. One stern "shhhh" and the entire group will quiet down and get back on task. But it only takes one parent to achieve this. More parents backstage will only cause problems.

If you are running a program in which the parents are paying a tuition fee for their children to attend classes and participate in plays, it will become even more vital for you to maintain a good relationship with the parents. Remember, they pay the bills. If they don't like you, chances are that they will not encourage the child to participate in your program. In order to keep your cash flow at a level to support your business, you must be nice to the customers, in this case the parents.

Although you must develop a good relationship with the parents, you should *never allow parents to attend rehearsals or to come backstage during a performance.*

Having parents backstage only makes the kids nervous. Parents won't be able to resist giving last minute advice, and this may go completely against what the director has told them. One mother insisted to her son before he went on stage that he stand up tall and speak loudly. His character called for him to slouch and muffle his words. Wanting to please the parent, the child decided to go against what he had learned in rehearsal and do what his parent wanted.

Parents backstage can cause all kinds of complications. They may delay the child from making an entrance, or give them the wrong cue or the wrong stage direction. Children need to be responsible for their own roles and not rely on Mom or Dad to help them out at the last minute.

Everyone wants to be a director—parents especially. Parents will naturally want their children to do their best. During rehearsals, I've had to maintain a permanent smile on my face to hide my gritting teeth as parents have given me advice on how to make my production just a little better. Directors should trust their own instincts. They don't need parents telling them what to do. Neither do the kids. You won't get a maximum rehearsal from children whose parents are watching. Kids need time to work out their character free from the critique of their parents. It is better to let cast members surprise their parents with the performance.

ACTIVITIES FOR INVOLVEMENT

As your program grows, so will your need for supportive parents. When I first started, I only had eleven children in my program. It was easy for me to handle rehearsals, and also build the set, and round up costumes and scenery. By the next summer, I had doubled my enrollment and there were that many more costumes and rehearsals. Luckily about that time, one mother appeared who was very interested in becoming involved. She offered to organize costumes and saved me hours on the phone by coordinating everyone's costume needs. Throughout the years, this mom has taken on more and more responsibility. Now that we have our own theater, she is an invaluable paid employee. She handles all our registration for classes, coordinates ticket sales, and oversees several office personnel. She did not have to be trained into the program. She has worked with me for ten years as a stage mom and, now that her own children are older, she has been able to take her volunteer work and turn it into a career.

So what can parents do to become involved? Here are just a few suggestions, although the list can be as long as the jobs involved in staging a production.

Office Work

Parents can handle your registrations for classes, ordering of scripts, stapling together of special copies of scenes, typing of the rehearsal schedule, telephoning of individuals when the rehearsal schedule must be changed, ordering of tickets, and the writing and typing of a program.

Advertising

Contacting potential advertisers for your program, placing newspaper and radio ads, and notifying the local cable station are just a few of the ways parents can help you advertise your production.

Ticket Sales

Your audience will probably be comprised primarily of friends and relatives of your cast members. Ask the parents to help you sell tickets. They may contact people they wouldn't normally have thought to invite. They could mention the play to their child's teacher. They can even call on area businesses and try to get them to order tickets for their employees.

Costuming

Parents can always be helpful in this area. You may be lucky enough to find a mom or dad who loves to sew and is eager to volunteer time; but even if they don't sew, parents can help in the costuming area. You may find a friendly mom or dad who enjoys going to garage sales, and can become your primary source for finding inexpensive costumes. Parents can make trips over to the material store; they can visit costume shops and help you get ideas for future productions. They can help by measuring children for their costumes, and handing out the costumes when they arrive.

Props
Finding props is like going on one gigantic scavenger hunt. Searching for the right props can be time consuming and frustrating. However, it can also be a lot of fun as you discover just the right chest to hold Long John Silver's gold. Many parents enjoy this aspect of theater and can save you time.

Set Construction
As long as you are in theater you will always need help with set construction. Parents often enjoy doing this with their kids. Schedule a Saturday morning set construction time and you may find you have an abundance of helpers.

Performance Day
On the day of a performance, you will need all kinds of help. As opening night draws near, parents who haven't been involved up to this point will probably be just as excited as their children. Put these parents to work. They can usher, hand out programs, or sell tickets at the door. For an added income, you may want to sell refreshments. Something as simple as juice and cookies is easy to prepare and can bring in a tidy sum.

THE ACTING PROGRAMS

Choosing the type of program you will offer your acting company can be challenging. The options are many. Will you offer a summer program only? Will your company be open only to elementary children, or will you have tots and high school students as well? Are you going to have acting classes only as an occasional workshop, or will they become an integrated part of your program? How many plays will you perform a year—one, two, five? Will you offer specialized classes such as makeup, clowning, dance, and singing? All of these decisions must be made before you advertise for participants in your program.

Throughout the years that I have taught acting, I've tried a variety of different programs. When I first started with my original eleven students, they were all different ages. The youngest was five and the oldest thirteen. There were four boys and seven girls. Together the younger ones learned from the older ones, and we formed a very close group, much like an old-fashioned, one room schoolhouse.

As the enrollment grew in my program, I thought that if I separated the children according to ages it might be easier to teach them. I then started a program for three different age levels. I had tots (ages four to six) in one group; younger elementary (ages seven through ten) in another group; and the middle school

Learning to operate the light board.

students (ages eleven through fifteen) in still another group. I staged larger productions with the older kids, and usually just put a quick one-act play together with the little ones. In the tots classes, I used mainly sensory perception exercises, and we did programs only for their parents. I continued this type of a program for about three years. During this time, I felt that while the tots program was successful, the elementary and middle school programs were lacking.

The middle school students were becoming too close of a group. They were very successful when they were on stage, but it wasn't turning out to be as positive as I would have liked. I felt that they were becoming very egotistical and a bit snobbish to new members joining the company. It was almost impossible to place a new fifth or sixth grader into the group because they instantly felt out of place. Most of the group had been together for several years and they felt no one could compete with them. Only the most talented were accepted within their ranks; other children dropped out quickly, feeling insecure.

The children in my younger group, ages seven through ten, weren't picking up the skills I wanted them too. In my beginning years, the younger children had learned by following the older ones. Now, there were no older ones in their classes to imitate and the growth rate for picking up valuable stage skills was slowing down.

A few years ago, I regrouped. Now, my classes are multi-age and multi-ability again. I try to keep enrollment in the classes at fifteen students. I place new students, no matter what their ages, in with a group of children who have already been with me for several years. A typical class load may consist of six or seven boys and eight or nine girls. Ages will vary. I may have two or three twelve-year olds, one eleven-year old, a ten-year old, two or three nine-year olds, four eight-year olds, two seven-year olds, and maybe even a six-year old who has completed the tot class. I always try to have at least one other child in the group in the same age range. For example, I would not put a twelve-year old in a class where the next oldest child was nine.

When I first regrouped, I expected rebellion among the ranks. I thought that the older kids would be completely against groupings with the younger ones. Instead, it made them feel important. They were the experts in their particular class. They also became the older brothers and sisters to the younger children in the class. Now, I really feel that the program is successful when we get together in a group and a little person crawls into the lap of one of the older kids.

TYPES OF PROGRAMS

Whatever program you choose, it must match not only the personalities of your company members but also your own interests and talents. Perhaps you have a special talent at clowning, or dancing, or singing. If you can write, you may want to perform only original plays. If you enjoy only working with older children, you may want to limit your enrollment to older grades. If you like teaching toddlers, you may want to add more tot classes. The following is just a sample of the types of programs you may want to run.

Children's Productions
In this type of a program you would have children audition to participate in a particular play. Generally, three to five productions are performed a year. With a large cast of 25 or more, the same children may or may not perform each time. A production fee is charged in which the children pay for the chance to perform. The fee also helps cover the cost of scripts, advertising, tickets, scenery, and props. Children are responsible for their own costumes.

School Year Acting Classes
This type of program is run as an extracurricular event during the school year. Parents pay a tuition fee to enroll their children in weekly acting classes. These classes can cover everything from

basic speaking to modeling. There should also be some movement involved. Although no formal production is planned, students should perform a small play or skit for their parents occasionally.

Children's Acting Company

This type of a program offers both classes and productions. Children may participate in the productions only if they are registered in the classes. There are no outside auditions. Each child is assigned to a basic acting class comprised of students of different sexes and ages. The classes meet once a week. The children also choose which plays each would like to participate in during the year. Parents pay one basic tuition fee which covers the cost of production. Costume fees are extra.

Summer Workshops

These types of workshops are generally designed for students interested in a more concentrated theater experience ending in a production. They can be arranged according to any age and usually last anywhere from two to four weeks. Parents pay one basic tuition fee for their children to experience a large variety of subjects in the performing arts.

Day Workshops

These are short specialty classes in a variety of subjects, such as clowning, juggling, dance, set design, lighting, and so on. Parents pay a tuition fee and students bring a lunch.

TYPES OF CLASSES

If you choose to begin a program in which you will offer classes, you will want to choose titles which are intriguing to your potential students. Once you have chosen the types of classes you will offer, put them together into an attractive brochure or flyer and distribute them to your potential students. The following are some examples of course descriptions which I have offered to my acting classes.

Clowning
Experiment with costumes, makeup, and zany skits in this crazy clowning class for elementary and middle school children.

Mini-Musical
Sing and swing your time away in this lively musical class. Guaranteed to make you kick up your heels and dance.

Technical Workshop
Learn the basics of set design, lighting, sound and set construction in this beginning technical workshop.

Movement, Music, and Mystery
This introductory theater class is for the littlest actors and actresses, ages five to seven. Music and art activities are incorporated here with beginning exercises in movement, creativity, and concentration.

Beginning Acting
Especially for the child new to acting, this beginning class will center around movement, mime, improvisation, and beginning dialogue.

Youth Acting
This class is designed for returning students. Through movement, music, exercises, and demonstrations, students will investigate areas essential to the performer. Emphasis is on development of individual style and creativity.

Storytelling
This class will center around the technique of storytelling. Students will learn how to master stories and intrigue their listeners through a series of theatrical techniques.

Summer Schedule

1991 Summer Classes
At the Stagedoor Performing Arts Center
formerly the Gem Theater

• Drama • Dance • Art •

Acting Classes
Instructor: Judy Hackbarth

• Stagedoor One •
Ages: Elementary & Middle School
Beginning acting class for newcomers.
Meets: Mon. & Wed. 9 - 10 am
Fee: $ 50

• Stagedoor Tots •
Ages: Preschool - Kindergarten
Introductory theater for the littlest
actors & actresses.
Meets: Mon. & Wed. 5:30 - 6:15 pm
Fee: $ 40

• Clowning •
Ages: Elementary & Middle School
Experiment with costumes, make-up &
zany skits in this clowning class.
Meets: Fri. 9:30 - 11:30 am
Fee: $ 50

• Technical Workshop •
Ages: Middle School & High School
Learn the basics of set design, lighting
& sound system operation.
Meets: Fri.. 12 - 1 pm
Fee: $ 25

• Mini-Musical •
Ages: Elementary & Middle School
Sing & swing the summer away in
this 'Salute to Sesame Street'
Meets: Tues. & Thur. 12:30 - 2:00 pm
Fee: $75

• Play Production •
Open to returning Stagedoor members
Celebrate our 10 year anniversary by
performing in 'Snow White'.
Meets: Mon. & Wed. 2 - 3:30 pm
Fee: $ 75

• Renaissance Performers •
By Audition Only
Class runs thru the fall. Performances
at the Minn. Renaissance Festival.
Meets: Mon. & Wed. 1 - 2 pm
Fee: $ 75

Call the Stagedoor
Center Box Office
to Register
• 246-4295 •

Dance Classes
Instructor: Gail Buell

• First Steps Ballet •
Ages: Pre-School
Beginning movement for the
tiniest dancers
Meets: Tues. & Thur. 9:30 - 10:00 am
Fee: $25

• Beginning Ballet •
Ballet class for the student new to dance.

Ages:	Meets:
5 - 7	Tues. & Thur. 10:15 - 11:00 am
8 - 10	Tues. & Thur. 11:15 - Noon
Pre-teen	Tues. & Thur. 5 - 6 pm
& teen	Fee: $50

Art Classes

• Anyone Can Draw •
Ages: Elementary & Middle School
Learn fundamentals of drawing or expand your
drawing skills in this versatile design class.
Meets: Mon. & Wed. 3:30 - 4:30 pm
Instructor: Kay Brathol Hostvet, Fee: $50

• Adding Color to Your Art •
Ages: Middle School
This class is designed to teach the basics of
working with color in art.
Meets: Mon. & Wed. 4:30 - 5:30 pm
Instructor: Kay Brathol Hostvet, Fee: $50

All Classes run from
June 17 - August 1
No classes the week of July 4th

• Marionette Making •
Ages: Elementary & Middle School
Create your own working puppet.
Perform a play with your marionettes
Meets: Mon. & Wed. 10 - 11 am
Instructor: Joan Wekander, Fee: $50

•• 1991 - 92 ••
Season Tickets
Now On Sale!

THE CLASSES

CHILDREN'S THEATER CLASSES

The key to children performing consistently and successfully on stage lies in the organization and teaching of classes in theater skills.

In the classes, group members are introduced to activities in creativity, group cohesion, movement, concentration, pantomime, improvisation, and dialogue development. These are all vital skills that children need to attain in order to achieve success on stage. Participation in the classes will also build up group rapport so that when the children are ready to perform they perform as a team, not as individuals trying to upstage each other.

WHY ACTING CLASSES?

Few children's theater companies offer classes to their participants. Generally, students audition for a play and rehearsals start immediately.

Offering classes is time-consuming. It is much easier to just begin rehearsing a play. It is in the classes, however, that the competencies in drama will be achieved. Once a group starts rehearsing a play, the time flies and students may be rotely performing things on stage successfully, but they will not remember the why's. Why should they watch their back on stage? Why should they project their voices? Why should they stay in character? If they do not remember the why's, they will repeat their errors in subsequent plays.

In acting class they learn the why's. The benefit of this is that rehearsals, then, become easier. Children will not have to be continually reminded to speak out. They will have learned in acting class why it is important to project. They will not have to be reminded to stay in character. They will have learned in acting class how to stay focused on stage.

Acting classes also hold children's interest in theater when they are not into production. It gives them continual theater activities to look forward to and helps them develop a peer group of children who have the same interests and talents.

ENROLLMENT IN THE CLASSES

When you sign up children for acting classes, you will want to get as diversified a group as possible. The worst scenario is to have all fifth-grade girls or only second- and third-graders in a class. On the stage, children will encounter a multitude of different characters. This should be true in acting classes also. Children of different ages, sexes, and ethnic backgrounds should be grouped together in acting classes. This will offer the class plenty of opportunities to experience a wide range of abilities and talents. Older children generally gain a score of self-confidence when they are the role models for the younger children. The younger children receive recognition from the older ones and strive to be like them.

A tots acting class.

Boys and girls who work together in acting class will become more comfortable with each other on stage. The first play I directed with my current theater group was *Snow White*. It took me three days to work through the scene where the Prince is expected to kiss Snow White. It is a vital scene in the play since it is the kiss which awakens Snow White from her sleep. The children I worked with in this play had no experience, and it was before I started offering classes. Everytime the Prince attempted to kiss Snow White he would dissolve in giggles, and no amount of threatening or cajoling could change the situation. Finally, I had them hide their faces so that they could fake the kiss.

Several years later, I directed *Tom Sawyer*. The children playing the parts of Tom and Becky had worked together in classes for several years. They mastered the kissing scene in one rehearsal and we had no other problems throughout the play. The experience of working together and feeling comfortable together in class assured the success of that scene on stage.

PROBLEM CHILDREN

Whenever you are dealing with a group of children you will occasionally encounter a child who is too loud, too quiet, too energetic, or too shy. You will meet children who constantly volunteer for every activity and children who refuse to try anything new.

To avoid encountering disciplinary problems in class, I suggest interviewing the children individually before they are allowed to enter the class. This interview will help you determine that they have made a choice to participate in classes and aren't being pressured by their parents to attend. If a child does not want to be somewhere, no amount of persuasion will change things. The child will be uncooperative and, ultimately, the entire class will suffer. This is really the core of all disciplinary problems.

Scheduling a quick chat with each child before classes start helps you get to know them better. You can establish class rules and discuss what the child's part in the class will be. The children can in turn tell you their expectations and desires. You will find out if the child is ready to be on stage or would prefer to stay in classes for a few weeks. You will also be able to discover the child's individual fears. Although children can be encouraged to try new activities, pushing them onto the stage before they are ready can ruin their own individual enjoyment of theater forever. Move slowly and accept children as individuals and you will rarely have discipline problems in class.

PLANNING A SCHEDULE

The best time to offer classes is once a week throughout the entire school year. However, when planning a class schedule, you must always keep in mind your production plan. Unless children are on vacation from school, they will have a difficult time attending

STAGEDOOR WINTER - SPRING SESSION

All classes meet once a week on either Monday, Tuesday, Wednesday, or Thursday. Please check the schedule below to find out when your class meets this semester.

Mon.	Tues.	Wed.	Thurs.
Jan. 6	Jan. 7	Jan. 8	Jan. 9
Jan. 13	Jan. 14	Jan. 15	Jan. 16
Jan. 20	Jan. 21	Jan. 22	Jan. 23

***Classes cancelled the weeks of Jan. 27-Feb. 7th for performances of Tumbleweeds.*

Feb. 10	Feb. 11	Feb. 12	Feb. 13

***Classes cancelled the week of Feb. 17th.-.School Break.*

Feb. 24	Feb. 25	Feb. 26	Feb. 27
Mar. 2	Mar. 3	Mar. 4	Mar. 5
Mar. 9	Mar. 10	Mar. 11	Mar. 12
Mar. 16	Mar. 17	Mar. 18	Mar. 19
Mar. 23	Mar. 24	Mar. 25	Mar. 26

***Classes cancelled the weeks of Mar. 30-Apr. 9th for performances of Raggedy Ann and Andy.*

Apr. 13	Apr. 14	Apr. 15	Apr. 16
Apr. 20	Apr. 21	Apr. 22	Apr. 23
Apr. 27	Apr. 28	Apr. 29	Apr. 30
May 4	May 5	May 6	May 7

***Week of May 11th-15th will be rehearsals for Parent's Night and Dance Recitals. These are tentatively scheduled for the 13th-17th of May.*

Stagedoor Players' schedule of classes for one semester.

rehearsals for a play and attending classes in the dramatic arts during the same week. Develop your class schedule around production times. This may mean that you offer classes two or three times a week when you are not rehearsing a play, and then halt the classes when the play goes into production. You can then resume classes when the play is over. This can develop into a schedule where students rehearse a play for four to six weeks, perform the play, attend off-production acting classes for three to four weeks, then begin rehearsing another play with the pattern continuing throughout the year. On the previous page is a sample calendar for my acting classes. This calendar covers one semester of classes.

There is no set pattern for offering classes. Whatever you decide, choose the schedule that works best for your group.

On the following pages, you will find activities that can take you through approximately thirty-two weeks of acting classes. This would comprise one full year. I always recommend starting slowly. Get the children comfortable with one another before you ask them to perform for each other. Once they have developed a rapport, they will be eager to "out-act" each other and you will be able to introduce more difficult activities.

The following part of this section is divided into seven parts. Each part deals with one specific skill children need to attain in order to achieve success on the stage. Lesson plans for each

Theater games help kids develop acting skills.

activity are detailed in a step-by-step order for the convenience of the instructor. A time sequence is recommended for each activity, but my advice on the time spent would be: if it is working, continue it!

CREATIVITY EXERCISES

Children are naturally creative creatures. They will see things that adults no longer have the ability to see, like imaginary friends and the pot of gold at the end of the rainbow. Often, the characters that we see on stage are very unlike real people. The situations portrayed may be unlike any experiences the normal person has ever had. In order to portray these characters and situations, the actors need to rely on their imaginations.

They need to pretend that they are that character they are portraying. Children are experts at pretending. They can create characters on stage that only the most talented adult actors would feel comfortable portraying.

Unfortunately, children are often taught in today's traditional schools to put most of their creativity on hold. Instead, they are encouraged to follow the rules and conform to the group. Lessons in creativity are important to help them keep in touch with their inner feelings. When we nurture a child's creativity, we are nurturing their inner talents. The following activities will help to keep children aware of how important creativity is on stage.

IMAGINE

Time: 30-45 minutes.

Materials: Paper, drawing pens, a record or tape player, an assortment of music.

1. Give each participant several sheets of blank paper and a drawing pen.

2. Ask them to close their eyes and listen to a selection of music. Allow one to two minutes of listening before asking them to explain what pictures they saw in their minds as they listened to the music. Encourage them to share their thoughts.

3. Discuss how everyone does not see the same picture in their mind. We all have different imaginations.

4. Play another selection and ask them to draw a picture of what they see in their minds while listening to the music.

5. Share the drawings orally and encourage differences in imagination.

6. After the participants have drawn several different selections, ask them to put the paper aside and move their bodies to the different types of music.

Try to use a wide variety of types of music in this exercise.

INKBLOTS

Time: 30 minutes.

Materials: Paper, pencils, inkblots.

1. Divide the group into smaller units of three or four.

2. Give each small group a piece of paper and pencil.

3. Distribute one inkblot to each group and have the group make a list of all of the things that they can see in the shape of the inkblot.

4. Have each individual group share their findings with the whole group.

Inkblots can be made by dropping a drop of ink on a piece of white paper and then creasing the paper in the middle.

SHADOWS

Time: 20-30 minutes.

Materials: Blank wall, bright spot light, large sheets of paper, crayons or marking pencils.

1. Explain to the group that you are going to experiment with making different kinds of shadows with your body.

2. Turn the bright light on the wall and demonstrate how they can make hand shadows.

3. Allow all of the members to experiment making hand shadows.

4. Turn on some lively music and invite the group to try making body shadows to the music.

5. Divide the group into pairs. Have one partner make a body shadow and have the other partner trace the shadow onto a large sheet of paper.

SHAPES

Time: 20 minutes.

Materials: Colored paper cut in different shapes, marking pens.

1. Give each participant a shape.

2. Have them study its shape.

3. Explain that there is more to the lines or shapes than they can see in the paper.

4. Ask them to take a marker and add their own ideas to the shape.

5. Have them share their hidden shapes with the group.

WHAT'S YOUR FEELING?

Time: 15 minutes.

Materials: Sets of ten or more pieces of construction paper cut in different shapes and sizes, whole construction paper, glue, one musical recording.

1. Give each participant one whole piece of construction paper and one set of pieces of construction paper. The glue should be accessible to everyone.

2. Listen to a musical selection.

3. As the group listens, instruct them to move the pieces of paper

around to show how the music makes them feel. They can move the pieces any way they want.

4. When the music stops they should paste down the design they have made.

5. Ask them to share their finished design with the class and explain their feelings.

COSTUME DESIGNERS

Time: 45 Minutes.

Materials: Pictures of stage costumes, newspapers, tape, scissors, colored markers or crayons, yarn or string.

1. Begin by showing the group pictures of costumes. These may be pictures from actual productions or pictures of patterns of costumes that can be made.

2. Ask each child to choose a character for whom they can create a costume.

3. Talk about the pieces of costume that that character might need. For example:

> Snow White - apron, cape, blouse, skirt, crown
> Raggedy Ann - dress, rag doll hair, apron
> Tin Soldier - uniform, hat, rifle
> Little Mermaid - swimming suit top, fish tail
> Dracula - tuxedo, cape
> Robin Hood - tunic, hat, bow and arrows

4. Show students the newspapers and tell them that you want them to use their imagination to create a costume for their character out of newspaper. They may also use tape, and string or yarn. They can add color with crayons, or markers, or even the comic pages.

5. Allow the students to work individually or in pairs.

6. After an ample amount of time, have a fashion show displaying the creations.

BOXES

Time: Two class sessions. The first session should be at least thirty minutes and the second session should be twenty minutes.

Materials: One brown grocery-size box for each child. These should vary in size. Tempera paint, paint aprons, lots of newspaper, paint brushes.

First Session:

1. Make sure you have ample room and clean-up materials for each child to have their own space to paint their cardboard box.

2. Encourage the children to be creative and paint designs or use different colors on their boxes.

Second Session:

1. Sit together in a circle and ask the children for possible uses for a cardboard box.

2. Ask the children to demonstrate how they would carry the box if it were filled with groceries, kittens, clothes, garbage, and other objects.

3. Using one box, ask a child to come forward and get into the box and pretend it is something else; for example, a car.

4. Ask other children to demonstrate, and let the group guess what the box could be for them. Examples here might include: a race car, a jack-in-the-box, a train, a boat.

5. After giving the children time to experiment individually with the boxes, combine two or three and ask what the boxes together could become.

6. Gradually add more boxes until all are being used. Perhaps they could build a giant mountain. Let all the children take turns knocking the mountain down.

BALLOONS

Time: 45 minutes.

Materials: Balloons for each child, a storybook that features a balloon story such as *The Valentine's Day Balloon Race*, a record or tape player, a record or tape featuring peppy music, face cutouts made from construction paper, glue.

1. Have the children sit in a circle in front of you on the floor and read a book on balloons. Discuss what it would feel like to be the balloon. How would your insides feel? Would you be heavy or light? Have they ever felt like a balloon?

2. Give a balloon to each child. Practice stretching the balloons. What do they feel like?

3. Try blowing up the balloon. What happens to our faces when we blow on the balloon? What happens to our stomachs as we blow on the balloon? Blow up the balloons and tie each one.

4. Turn on the music and ask the children to hit their balloons into the air as they listen to the music.

5. When they have all had a chance to hit their balloon for a few minutes, they should gather together in a circle. Is it difficult to keep your balloon in the air? What did that balloon feel like?

6. Ask the children to pretend they have an imaginary balloon. Practice blowing up the imaginary balloons (note facial expressions). Practice hitting the imaginary balloon to music.

7. Have the children become the balloon. They should get their bodies very small and then blow themselves up. They should get gradually bigger and bigger until they can float around the room.

8. Divide the group into three's. Have one child be the balloon and the other two take turns hitting the balloon softly back and forth.

For a follow-up activity give each child a large balloon with several precut face pieces and have them glue the faces onto the balloon. Each child should be encouraged to make an unusual face. Have them give names to their balloon people.

MARSHMALLOW PEOPLE

Time: 30 Minutes.

Materials: Large bag of large marshmallows, large bag of small marshmallows, toothpicks.

1. Have the students sit in a circle and give each one a large marshmallow. (They should be encouraged NOT to eat their marshmallow.)

2. Discuss what the marshmallows smell like.

3. Discuss what the marshmallows feel like.

4. What sounds do marshmallows make?

5. Discuss the uses of marshmallows.

6. Have them take a lick and then a small bite. What does a marshmallow taste like? Tell them to close their eyes and eat the marshmallow.

7. Imagine that there is a large marshmallow in the center of the group.

8. Select one student to step inside the imaginary marshmallow. Describe what it feels like.

9. Ask everyone to step inside the marshmallow. What happens?

For a follow-up activity, give the children marshmallows and toothpicks and see what they can create?

POPCORN PEOPLE

Time: 45 minutes.

Materials: Unpopped popcorn, popcorn maker, salt, butter, syrup, bowls, wet cloths, napkins.

l. Begin by passing around unpopped kernels of popcorn and asking the children to identify them. Ask the children to touch and feel the kernels. Look for descriptive words to describe them.

2. Place unpopped popcorn in an automatic popcorn maker and begin popping. Ask the students to listen quietly. Have them close their eyes for a time and imagine the kernels popping. What smells do they smell?

3. When the popcorn is finished, pass around a small bowl to each child. Ask them NOT to eat it but just to smell and examine the different kernels.

4. Ask the student to taste one kernel. What does it taste like?

5. Ask the students if they would like butter or syrup on their popcorn. Place toppings on individual popcorn servings. Eat the popcorn.

6. When everyone has finished eating, ask the students to take space around the floor and pretend they are a kernel of unpopped popcorn.

7. Begin by pretending that the floor is the hot part of a range. All the children can crouch until the stove is turned on.

8. Explain that the floor is becoming hotter and hotter, and finally, they begin to pop. Instruct them to stop popping when they think they are a full kernel.

9. Once they have finished popping, they can imagine a topping that is being poured over them.

GROUP COHESION ACTIVITIES

Group cohesion activities are important for building up a connection among your young actors and actresses. An important factor in being a member of a professional acting company is the feeling of pride you have in your troupe. If there is a feeling of friendliness and an eagerness to be together that surrounds the company, you are more likely to have a successful program. The following activities will allow your group to have fun together, while teaching them the importance of working together to accomplish a common goal.

LET'S DANCE

Time: 20-30 minutes.

Materials: A record or tape player and music.

1. Divide the group into male-female partners. Have the partners stand opposite from each other in a long line. Instruct the group that when the music starts they should walk forward, toward each other for four steps. They should then walk backward four steps.

2. Next, they walk forward four steps, join right hands with their partner, turn once around clockwise, and then return to their original places.

3. They walk forward, join left hands and turn counterclockwise before returning to their original places.

4. Walk forward and meet their partner, join both hands, and turn once around clockwise before returning to their places.

5. Walk forward, meet their partner and do-si-do by passing right shoulders, passing back to back, passing left shoulders, and then passing backwards to their original places.

6. While the other couples clap in time to the music, the first couple join hands and pass down the line between the other couples. They slide eight steps down and eight steps back to their original place.

7. The first couple hook right elbows and turn one and a half times around clockwise. The first girl goes to the second boy in line while the first boy goes to the second girl in line. They swing their new partners once around and then meet in the center and swing each other.

8. The first couple goes down the line swinging first the next person in line and then back to swing their original partner. When they have finished swinging each person down the line, they meet at the end and slide back to their original places.

9. The first couple split and each leads their line down to the end of the set where they join hands and form an arch. The other couples come through the arch. The second couple becomes the head of the set and the dance repeats until the music stops.

This dance, which is a form of the Virginia Reel, may be danced to any type of music. It is fun to start with traditional square-dance music and then gradually switch to rock music.

EN GARDE!

Time: 20-30 minutes.

Materials: None.

1. Ask members of the group to remove their shoes.

2. Have the two smallest members of the group come forward and have a toe wrestling match.

3. The winner of the match challenges the next tallest person.

4. Continue with the challenges until everyone has had a chance to toe wrestle.

Toe wrestling is the same as hand wrestling. The winner is the first person to successfully place his or her foot on top of the opponents foot and hold it down until the count of ten.

GUESS WHO?

Time: 15-20 minutes.

Materials: Name tags of famous personalities.

1. When participants arrive, give them a name tag of a famous personality.

2. Pin the name tag on their back.

3. Instruct the participants that they must discover whose name tag they are wearing by asking other members of the group "yes" and "no" questions.

Try to choose personalities that are popular with children, such as Donald Duck, Miss Piggy, and other television and movie characters.

CATCH ME IF YOU CAN

Time: 15 minutes.

Materials: One scarf.

1. Ask group members to form a long line, each holding on to the hand of the person in front of them.

2. Tuck a scarf into the back waistband of the last player in the line.

3. At a given signal, the first member of the group must try to grab the scarf from the last player.

4. When the first member succeeds, he or she then moves to the end of the line and becomes the last player with the scarf.

This game can get very wild. Play it in a large open area. Instruct students that if the line breaks before the scarf is captured they are to stop immediately.

Stagedoor kids "take a seat" in a group cohesion exercise.

HAVE A SEAT

Time: 15-20 minutes.

Materials: Enough chairs for each member of the group.

1. Place chairs in one long line with all of them facing in the same direction.

2. Ask all group members to take a seat.

3. Give the following instructions to the group: "Everyone having blonde hair move over one seat."

4. If that characteristic applies to any of the group members, they should move over one chair. If someone is sitting in that chair, they should sit on their lap. The person sitting in the last chair in the line moves to the first chair in the line.

5. Whenever a chair is empty, the group leader removes it from the line.

6. Play continues with the leader calling out different characteristics: blue ribbon, freckles, white tennis shoes, and so forth.

7. The game ends when there is only one chair remaining and everyone is sitting on it.

Remind players when you start this game that they should be very careful not to "squash" someone too hard.

TRUST SPINS

Time: 20 minutes.

Materials: None.

1. Ask group members to sit on the floor and form a tight circle.

2. Have each member of the group remove their shoes.

3. Select one person to stand in the center of the circle.

4. Group members are to place their feet tightly around the ankles of the person in the middle.

5. Tell the group that they are to hold their arms out straight in

front of them with their palms pointing toward the person in the middle.

6. On the count of three, the person in the center stiffens up and falls forward.

7. Members of the group keep the person from falling and work together to spin the person around the circle. Ask the group members to keep their arms and legs rigid. The person in the middle must also have his or her body rigid for this to work effectively.

8. When the person in the middle falls, the person he or she falls on goes into the middle to receive the spin.

TRUST FALLS

Time: 15 minutes.

Materials: None.

1. The group stands in two lines facing inward.

2. Each person holds their arms outright and connects them with the person opposite, holding firmly.

3. The line should be forming a long bed.

4. One person stands on a table at the end of the line.

5. On the count of three, the person on the table stiffens and falls forward into the outstretched arms.

6. This can continue until each member of the group has had a chance to fall.

Make certain that group members understand the importance of working closely together on this activity. One group member not doing his or her part may cause the falling group member to hit the floor instead of the nice, soft member-made bed.

TANGLES

Time: 15-30 minutes.

Materials: None.

1. Instruct all participants to stand in a tight circle and place their hands toward the center.

2. Next, participants are to close their eyes and then grab onto another person's hands.

3. Before the group reopens their eyes, check to make sure that no one holds both hands with the same person or holds the hand of a person right next to them.

4. On the count of three the group should open their eyes and attempt to untangle themselves into a perfect circle without letting go of hands.

For this to work more effectively, you may want to appoint one person to be the untangler and take charge of solving this human puzzle.

BLOW-UPS

Time: 15 minutes.

Materials: None.

1. Have the group sit in a circle while you introduce the game.

2. Ask one person to demonstrate how he or she can pretend to explode his or her body.

3. Ask several other people to demonstrate their own explosions.

4. Select one person to be the explosion judge.

5. Tell the group that they are going to be playing a normal game of tag within a small area.

6. When they are tagged, they must blow-up or explode in a dramatic way and then sink to the floor.

7. The explosion judge will determine if their explosion was dramatic enough. If it was, they can go back into the game; if it wasn't, they must wait on the sidelines until the next game begins.

This is an excellent game to bring out the shy child. Generally, as the game continues, even the shyest children will perform loud explosions to get back into the game.

TREASURE HUNT

Time: 20 Minutes.

Materials: Clues for the treasure hunt (one set of clues for each group); a treasure for each group to find (candy or small toys).

1. Divide the children into two or three groups.

2. Give each group a set of clues to find a treasure. (The clues should be different for each group and lead to a different spot.)

3. Each group should then try to find the treasure hidden around the room or building.

4. Upon finding the treasure, the group shares the treats.

Clues might read:

> Finding the treasure is all the rage.
> Look for a clue hidden on the . . . (st*age)*

> Find this clue if you are able.
> It's hidden beneath the old prop . . . *(table)*

> To find the treasure you won't need a map.
> A clue is hidden in the . . . *(trap)*

MOVEMENT FUN

On stage, children are often called upon to do a part that feels embarrassing or abnormal. They might be asked to be the slightly crazy wicked witch who torments Snow White or perhaps one of the dancing jitterbugs in *The Wizard of Oz.* How successfully the actor or actress portrays the characteristics of an unusual personality will depend on how the audience receives the performance. If an actor is stiff in the part, the audience will have a hard time believing him and the entire production will suffer. The movement exercises included in this section are helpful in teaching children to communicate with their entire body. Movement is also an excellent way to help a child get in touch with his or her own creative energy. Too often children are encouraged to sit still and learn intellectually instead of creatively. These activities will help to make them more aware of their own inner feelings and imaginations. Ultimately, a good performer is one who has a highly active imagination!

BODY MELTS

Time: 10-15 minutes.

Materials: A small drum or tambourine.

1. Discuss with the group how a snowman or icicle melts slowly.

2. Ask for a volunteer to show how a snowman might melt in the hot sun.

3. Practice melting with the entire group.

4. Ask players to walk around the room to the beat of the drum. When the drum stops, they should slowly melt to the ground.

This is a wonderful activity to use with younger children.

MORE BODY MELTS

Time: 10-15 minutes.

Materials: A record or tape player and lively music.

1. Play lively music and allow the group to move around the room in a circle pattern. Instruct them that when the music stops they are to freeze.

2. Stop the music. Unfreeze each player by tapping them lightly on the head. When they are unfrozen, they should slowly melt to the ground.

Choose music which makes the group want to move quickly about. That way when you stop the music their movements will have to stop quickly.

MONSTER MELTS

Time: 10-15 minutes.

Materials: None.

1. Have the group form a line facing in one direction.

2. Ask members of the group to show their most horrid monster faces.

3. One at a time, starting at the right side of the line tell the group you want them to jump up and make their most horrible monster face, and then freeze.

4. Proceed down the line having each member freeze into their most horrible monster face. When the entire line is frozen ask them to relax and become normal faces again.

Monsters in movement class.

5. Ask each member of the group to think up a name which describes their terrible monster face.

6. Tell them you want them to jump up and yell out their monster's name as they form the monster face again. They should freeze when they have done this.

7. Proceed down the line again.

8. Repeat this process, but when the last person in the line has frozen as a monster ask that person to melt to the floor.

9. Reverse the process down the line with each monster melting to the ground.

Encourage the monster faces to be as horrible as possible.

ONE, TWO, THREE

Time: 15 minutes.

Materials: None.

1. Ask the group to line up on the front of the performing area facing outward.

2. Starting at the beginning of the line, have each person yell out a number: one, two, three, etc.

3. Have the group form their bodies into the smallest positions they can.

4. When all are in position, have them, one at a time, jump up and put their body in the biggest position they can while they shout out their number. When this is done, they should freeze in position.

5. When all members of the group are frozen, have the last number melt to the ground and so forth until number one is melted.

6. Repeat this process having group members yell their numbers in different moods, such as sad, angry, afraid, and happy.

A variation on this is to have them yell out letters or made-up names instead of numbers.

BRIDGES

Time: 10-15 minutes.

Materials: None.

1. Stand at one side of the room.

2. Explain that you are going to help the group span the room by forming a human bridge.

3. Ask one player to come forward and arrange his or her body into some type of a bridge that must be climbed over or crawled under.

4. When the first player is in position, bring up another player and ask him or her to go over or under the first player, and then get into position themselves next to the first player. Each player should join the bridge by also placing his or her body into a position which can be climbed over or crawled under.

5. Continue adding players to build the bridge across the room.

6. When all players have become a part of the bridge, have the first player crawl over or under the bridge to the opposite side of the room.

7. All players follow the first member until all members of the group are on the opposite side of the room.

This game works best if played in a long room.

BODY MOVES

Time: 10-15 minutes.

Materials: A record or tape player and lively music.

1. Ask the group to listen carefully to your verbal instructions

while the music is playing.

2. Start the music and tell the group they may dance about the room.

3. Abruptly stop the music and yell "freeze." Everyone must stop in whatever position they are in and freeze their body like a statue.

4. Restart the music but tell the group that they may only dance by moving their arms.

5. After a brief period again yell "freeze."

6. Tell the group that when you restart the music they may move only their heads.

7. Repeat the stopping, freezing, and starting process, instructing the group each time to move different parts of their bodies.

Allow the music to play for a few minutes before yelling "freeze." It is better if the freeze command is unexpected.

LET'S TAKE A WALK

Time: 15 minutes.

Materials: A record or tape player and several selections of lively music.

1. Gather the group on one side of the room.

2. Start the music and have one player walk to the other side of the room. Encourage the player to let the music guide his or her

movements. The player may want to skip, run, dance, or do an unusual step to the music.

3. When the player returns back to the starting point, he should tap another player. The tapped player follows the first player back across the room, mimicking his movements.

4. When both players arrive back at the starting point, they tap two more people who then follow them in the same movements across the room.

5. This continues until the whole group is walking identically across the room.

6. When all have crossed, pick another leader, change the music, and repeat the process.

Encourage the players to use bizarre movements. They can walk like an old man, walk with a shuffle, walk like a rap dancer. The stranger the movements, the more fun this activity becomes.

ROOM CROSSES

Time: 15-20 minutes.

Materials: None.

1. Discuss with the group the many different ways they can cross a room.

2. Ask one member of the group to demonstrate. (He or she may choose to walk, run, skip, etc.)

3. Now, ask another member to demonstrate a different method of

crossing the room. This must be a different style from the first player.

4. Continue sending group members across the room, but each one must cross in a different manner.

5. Try to see how many different ways the group can think of to cross a room.

Suggested ways to cross the room: without feet touching the floor, tip toe, backwards, on one foot, with eyes closed, jumping, skipping, twirling, sliding on stomach, walking on their hands, and rolling.

STREAMERS

Time: 5-10 minutes.

Materials: Crepe paper streamers (2 per player), lively music.

1. Give two streamers to each player.

2. Play lively music that portrays a variety of emotions.

3. Ask the players to move around the room to the music using their streamers to create birds, butterflies, or just circles in the wind.

To make this more interesting, vary the speed and volume of the music.

GRAB THAT TAIL!

Time: 10-15 minutes.

Materials: One scarf per player.

1. Give each player a scarf to tuck in the back of their waistband. They should leave at least two-thirds of the scarf hanging down.

2. At a given signal, all players try to grab each other's scarves.

3. When a player loses his scarf, he must give all of his captured scarves to that player. The scarfless player then sits out until the game restarts.

This makes a fun warm-up game.

CONCENTRATION GAMES

The ability to focus into one's character on stage and eliminate all distractions can be a difficult task for young children. They may have all the good intentions in the world, but when they see Mom and Dad sitting in the front row they have a hard time remembering that they are supposed to be the Queen of Hearts or the Mad Hatter. Instead, they think "Mom's watching. I hope my costume is on right."

Concentration exercises will help children to stay in character while on stage. These activities will also help them learn how to stay focused on the performance when audience distractions begin.

QUIET PLEASE!

Time: Varies.

Materials: Kitchen timer.

1. The group sits in a circle.

2. Tell the group that they will be building up their ability to concentrate on being perfectly quiet.

3. Set the kitchen timer for 15 seconds. The group sits quietly until the timer goes off.

4. Gradually increase the time until the group can sit for five minutes.

This makes a good beginning exercise.

STARING CONTESTS

Time: 5-10 minutes.

Materials: None.

1. Divide the group into pairs.

2. Each pair stands facing each other with arms either folded or at their sides.

3. At a beginning signal, they lock eyes and stare at each other.

4. The staring continues until one member of the pair looks away. When that happens, the pair must sit down.

5. The last pair standing and staring wins.

This game should be played before attempting to play Mirrors.

MIRRORS

Time: 10-15 minutes.

Materials: None.

1. The group pairs off in twos.

2. Each pair stands facing each other.

3. One person of each group is selected to be the leader.

4. The pairs are instructed to stare into each other's eyes during this exercise.

5. At a given signal, the leaders begin by making movements with their hands while continuing to stare into their partner's eyes.

6. The partner must echo the movements as though they were looking in a mirror.

7. This continues with one person being the leader until they have mastered it. Then, they switch leaders and repeat.

Gradually, the leaders may want to add facial expressions or leg movements to the mirror picture.

Ripple mirrors improve concentration.

RIPPLES

Time: 10-15 minutes.

Materials: None.

1. Begin with one pair of actors doing mirrors.

2. Choose another pair of actors to stand directly behind the first pair.

3. The second pair should mirror the actions of the first pair.

4. Gradually, add more and more actors to each side. The result will be a ripple of each mirror movement.

Instruct participants to focus on the person directly in front of them. Most people will try to mirror the person at the head of the line.

REPETITIONS

Time: 15-20 minutes.

Materials: None.

1. Instruct the group to stand in a circle.

2. One player starts by making a noise and simple movement. (Example: A player may extend a fist and yell "pow.")

3. The next group member repeats this sound and action and adds another.

4. This continues around the circle with everyone repeating the previously made sounds and actions and then adding to them.

5. If a player forgets the sequence of movements, he or she must sit down.

6. Continue around the circle several times until there is only one player who remains standing.

Encourage group members to be creative in their sounds and actions.

MAKE A NOISE!

Time: 15-20 minutes.

Materials: None.

1. The group gathers in a circle.

2. One player begins by putting a sound together with a motion. For example, raising a fist and yelling "POW!"

3. Everyone in the group repeats this sound.

4. The next player makes another sound and motion, such as stomping a foot and yelling "ZIP!"

5. The group repeats this sound and also the first sound.

6. The next member adds another sound and movement which the group repeats.

7. The group also repeats this and the first sound.

8. This action continues around the circle as each of the players add their own motion and sound.

This game is effective if the leader encourages the players to go very fast.

TENNIS BALL CHALLENGE

Time: 20-30 minutes.

Materials: 12 tennis balls.

1. The group sits in a circle.

2. The leader calls out the name of someone in the circle and then rolls them one tennis ball.

3. The person who receives the ball then calls out the name of someone else in the circle and rolls the same tennis ball to that person.

4. This continues around the circle until everyone has had the ball.

5. After the ball has been around the circle once, the leader tells the group that they will repeat the same sequence but a little faster.

6. When this is done, the leader then tells the group that they will repeat the sequence again, but this time a second ball will start once the first ball is on its way.

7. Gradually, the leader introduces more balls one right after the other in the same sequence until twelve balls can successfully be passed at the same time.

Encourage the players to remember who they roll the ball to and who rolls the ball to them. They should refrain from calling out someone else's name.

DO YOU HEAR WHAT I HEAR?

Time: 15-20 minutes.

Materials: None.

1. Divide the group into pairs. Each pair sits facing each other.

2. One member of the pair makes a sound and the other player must repeat that sound as closely as possible.

3. This continues for several minutes; then, the actors reverse roles.

You may want to try using a tape recorder so that the players can hear how closely they mimick the original sounds.

IT'S RAINING!

Time: 10-15 minutes.

Materials: None.

1. Instruct the group to sit in a circle.

2. The leader starts by slowly rubbing his hands together to simulate the sound of rain.

3. The person on the right of the leader then takes up the same movement and so on around the circle until the person to the left of the leader receives the movement.

4. When the sound comes back to the leader (and everyone else is still doing it), the leader starts another sound around. The next sound should indicate rain getting louder. It can be fingers snapping or a light tapping of the foot.

5. The second sound replaces the first sound as it works its way around the circle.

6. When the second sound comes back to the leader, he then begins another storm sound such as a loud clap to indicate thunder. This sound then continues around the circle.

7. To end the rainstorm, the leader gradually sends softer noises around the circle until finally he places his hands in his lap and waits for that motion to work its way around the circle.

This is a fun exercise to do during the Halloween season. You can even add in a cat meowing and a witch's cackle.

LET'S TALK!

Time: 15-20 minutes.

Materials: None.

1. Divide the group into threes. Number the participants in each group: one, two, and three.

2. Player number one in each group chooses a subject and begins to talk to player number two about it as if player three is not present.

3. Player number three chooses a subject and also begins to talk to player two about it as if player one was not present.

4. Player two must keep a conversation going with both people at the same time without letting either player sit and wait.

5. Conversation should continue for approximately three to five minutes.

The subjects chosen must be ones that lend themselves to in-depth discussion.

WHO IS IT?

Time: 10-15 minutes.

Materials: Blindfold.

1. One player is brought before the group and blindfolded.

2. Another member of the group comes forward and speaks to him or her in a disguised voice.

3. The blindfolded person is given three chances to guess who it is.

This should be played after the group has met several times and is familiar with other players' voices.

RECITATIONS

Time: 15-20 minutes.

Materials: None.

1. One participant is asked to come forward and recite a short nursery rhyme.

2. When the first participant has demonstrated proficiency at reciting a poem, another person is brought forward and asked to recite another poem.

3. When both participants can recite their poems correctly, they are

asked to turn their backs to each other and each recite their own poem at the same time.

4. Once the players have mastered reciting poems at the same time with their backs to each other then they are asked to face each other and recite their poems.

5. Gradually, more people and more poems are introduced until the entire group is reciting different nursery rhymes at the same time.

This activity takes lots of practice to do correctly. Start slowly!

HAND ME A LINE!

Time: 15-20 minutes.

Materials: None.

1. Assemble the group in a circle.

2. The leader whispers a simple sentence into one member's ear and that member in turn whispers it to the person on the right and so on around the circle.

3. The last person in the circle says the sentence out loud to see if it stayed intact around the circle.

4. Repeat the process with another sentence.

Try to gradually make the sentences more complex as the game continues. A sample sentence might be: The wicked witch wrestled the wrinkled old wizard to the ground.

WHO BEGAN?

Time: 15-20 minutes.

Materials: None.

1. Assemble the players in a circle.

2. One person is selected to be the investigator and is sent from the room.

3. When the investigator is gone, the group selects one person to be the leader.

4. This leader begins a movement such as finger snapping or whistling and the other group members copy it. The leader will change the movement several times.

5. The investigator is brought back into the room and must determine who began the movement.

6. Play continues until the investigator successfully guesses the leader.

7. Choose another investigator and begin again.

The leader should be able to change the movement several times before the investigator guesses.

CHANGES

Time: 15-20 minutes.

Materials: None.

1. Divide the group into pairs.

2. Give players two minutes to carefully observe the players opposite them. They should note clothes, hairstyle, etc.

3. Have the players turn their backs to each other.

4. Each player should change three things about themselves. They may untie a shoe, switch a watch from left to right arm, etc.

5. Players face each other again.

6. Each player must identify what changes their partner made.

7. Change partners and go to four changes.

8. Keep changing partners until you can get up to eight changes.

You may want to have a box of accessories ready for players to wear before the game starts. This will make the eight changes easier.

CATCH THE CANE

Time: 10-15 minutes.

Materials: A cane.

1. All players form a circle with one member in the center.

2. Give each player a number.

3. The center player has a cane that is held upright on the floor.

4. The center player releases the cane and at the same time calls out a number held by one of the other players.

5. The player whose number is called has to catch the cane before it falls to the floor.

6. If the player succeeds in catching the cane he or she trades places with the center player.

7. Continue until several players have had a chance to be in the middle.

PANTOMIME PLAY

Pantomime is performing without words. This is a wonderful way to introduce children to acting. In pantomime, children must concentrate on communicating their message without the convenience of language. Everything must be made clear through the use of body and facial expression. Often children beginning in acting are embarrassed at revealing their real personalities through dialogue. They fear that they won't sound like the character should. They worry that they won't be loud enough. Pantomime frees them of these restrictions and allows them to concentrate solely on their performance.

Communicating an idea and acquiring stage skills are the basis for the following exercises. The basics of good pantomime—consistency, concentration, exaggerated expression, and gesture, are important and should be stressed. However, learning to relax on stage and acquiring creativity skills are equally important in

Pantomime activities help to develop acting ability.

preparing children for stage presentations. The pantomime activities suggested here will help children feel more comfortable with their acting talents. The gradual progression of acting techniques encountered in pantomime will build the skills they will eventually need to portray a wide range of characters on stage.

RELAXATION JOURNEY

Time: 10 Minutes.

Materials: None.

1. Ask each of the children to find space in the room where they can lie on their backs. They should not be close enough to touch each other.

2. Explain that relaxation is a very important part of acting.

3. Ask the children to close their eyes and imagine themselves on this relaxation journey. They should act out whatever motions are asked for in the story.

4. Read the following:

Spread out and find your own space. Make sure you have enough room to make snow angels. Now, take a moment and feel the weight of your body. Your entire body should feel very heavy, it just sinks into the floor. Think about your feet. They are so heavy. Your ankles, legs, and knees all feel really heavy. Concentrate on how heavy your fingers are becoming. Your wrists, arms, and now your entire body feels so heavy. Feel the weight. Imagine you are lying on the beach, in the hot sand. The sun is beating down and you feel completely relaxed. Just feel the warmth as it overtakes each part of your body.

Now, you feel a cool breeze as it comes up and lightens up each part of you. You can feel yourself slowly floating upward. You float above the sand and can look down and see your imprint below. Then you float up higher and higher. Imagine looking down. What do you see? Clouds, colors?

As the breeze carries you along, you travel high above all of your favorite places. Where are you going? Is it to the beach, to the mountains, or to the country? What do you see below you?

You continue to float until you enter completely into the clouds. Everywhere you look there are clouds. What color are they? Are they pink, yellow, or white? They feel soft and your body continues to relax.

Now, you start to slowly float back down to your place on the warm sand. You can feel your body becoming heavier as it settles on land once again. When the sun beats down on you this time, it seems to touch each part of your body. As it touches your toes, you tense. Then relax. Your ankles tense, then relax. Concentrate on each body part. It touches your knees, tense, relax. Legs, tense, relax. Hips, tense, relax.

Now as I say each part hold it tense. Toes, ankles, knees, legs, hips, chest, fingers, wrists, elbows, arms, shoulders, neck, head. Hold your body very tense. And now release slowly your head, neck, shoulders, arms, elbows, wrists, fingers, chest, hips, legs, knees, ankles, toes. Relax. Take a deep breath and release.

Let your body sink into the floor. Feel the relaxation. Slowly roll lightly to the left, now to the right.

When you are ready, stand up slowly. Keep your eyes closed and your body bent over. Then, slowly stand straight up, stretch, and relax.

EXPRESSIONS

Time: 15 minutes.

Materials: None.

1. Divide the children into groups of no more than five or six.

2. Ask one group at a time to come forward and turn their backs to the others.

3. Explain that this group is onstage, and, on the count of three, you would like them to turn around and pantomime a feeling. Explain that in pantomime they can use no sounds.

4. Count to three, and ask the group to pantomime:

> Anger
> Sadness
> Happiness
> Excitement
> Embarrassment

5. Change groups and repeat until all children have been before each group.

6. Continue in this way, alternating groups and doing five feelings at a time. Other feelings to use might include:

> Sleepy
> Nervous
> Scared
> Silly
> Unsure
> Sick
> Hot
> Cold
> Carefree
> Uptight

PANTOMIME ACTIVITIES

Time: 20 minutes.

Materials: None.

1. Divide the children into groups of no more than five or six.

2. Ask one group at a time to come forward and turn their backs to the others.

3. Explain that this group is onstage, and, on the count of three, you would like them to turn around and pantomime an activity.

4. Count to three, and ask them to individually pantomime the following:

> Peeling a banana
> Unwrapping gum, chewing it, and blowing a bubble
> Combing their hair
> Pitching a baseball
> Petting a cat

5. Change groups and repeat until all children have been before each group.

6. Continue in this way, alternating groups and doing five activities at a time. Other activities to use might include:

> Chopping down a tree
> Painting a wall
> Pulling a wagon
> Playing tennis
> Finding a dollar bill
> Putting up an umbrella
> Shoveling snow

THE PANTOMIME WALK

Time: 20 minutes.

Materials: A record or tape player and an assortment of lively music.

1. Divide the children into groups of no more than five or six.

2. Ask one group at a time to come forward and turn their backs to the others.

3. Explain that this group is onstage, and, on the count of three, you would like them to turn and walk towards the front of the stage (or else across the room) as a character.

4. Count to three, and ask them to pantomime the following character walks:

> Robot
> Old man or old woman
> Ballet dancer
> Baby
> Roller skater

5. Change groups and repeat until all children have been before each group.

6. Continue in this way, alternating groups and doing five characters at a time. Other characters to use might include:

> Baseball player
> King

Drunk
Young child
Soldier
Tennis player
Indian
Tightrope walker

MUSIC PANTOMIMES

Time: 30 Minutes.

Materials: A record or tape player and an assortment of different types of music. (The music should be instrumental only.)

1. Choose one child to come forward. Explain that you are going to start some music and you would like the child to pick an activity to do to the music. The activity may be very simple, such as sweeping the floor, pounding a nail, or wrapping a gift.

2. Start the music and have the student pantomime his or her chosen activity.

3. While the first player is pantomiming, choose another student to join in pantomiming a related activity. They may not do the same activity but must do something that would be done in the same general setting. For example, if the first player is sweeping the floor, the second player could vacuum or dust.

4. Continue to add children into the pantomime. Each should introduce a new activity although all of them should work together on the chosen task.

5. The pantomime continues until the music ends.

6. Restart the activity with another selection of music.

SITUATIONAL PANTOMIMES

Time: 30 Minutes.

Materials: Slips of paper with situations written on them.

1. Ask the children to sit in a group in front of a performing area. They will be the audience as each member of the group comes forward to perform.

2. Give each child a slip of paper with a situation written on it. Explain that they are not to show the paper to anyone.

3. Ask one child to come forward and pantomime his or her situation.

4. The other children can guess what is happening.

5. Stop the children if they are not using very specific movements. You may want to comment on how they can improve. For example, if the slip of paper says "washing the dishes" ask: Where is the dish washing soap? Where are the faucets for the water? Where is the sink stopper?

Some examples of situations might be:

> Washing the dishes
> Cooking pancakes
> Sewing a button on a shirt
> Sweeping the floor
> Diapering a baby

Putting on roller skates
Getting ready to bat in a baseball game
Walking a dog
Planting a garden

BASEBALL GAME

Time: 20 minutes.

Materials: Plastic bat and nerf ball.

1. Select half of the group to become two separate baseball teams with at least five to six on a team.

2. The remaining members of the group will be the spectators.

3. While the two teams play an inning of "real" baseball, the remaining members of the group should watch carefully, paying special attention to facial and body movements.

4. After one inning of play, ask the spectators to replace the players and play the game again. But this time, they play the game without the real ball and bat. Instead, they pantomime movements.

This is a good activity for a large group. You can add as many players and spectators as you want.

THE TUG-OF-WAR

Time: 20-30 minutes.

Materials: One long sturdy rope.

1. Ask two members of the group to come forward. Hand each member an end of the rope and ask them to have a tug-of-war.

2. While they are competing, ask the members of the group to observe their body and facial expressions.

3. After a few minutes, ask these two members to sit down and select two more group members to come up and pantomime the tug-of-war that they have just seen.

4. During the pantomime, ask the group to coach the players in their facial expressions and body movements to get as close to the real action as possible.

Stagedoor kids pantomime a tug-of-war.

5. Next, bring up four players, two per side of the rope. Repeat the tug-of-war. Again, ask the group members to observe facial expressions and body movements. They should also observe how the two players on each side must work together.

6. After a few minutes replace the real group with the observers who once again pantomime the situation using an imaginary rope.

7. Gradually, add more group members until the entire class is involved in an imaginary tug-of-war.

Pay special attention to placement of the hands on the imaginary rope. They must be coordinated per team to seem realistic.

THE ORCHESTRA

Time: 15 Minutes.

Materials: A record player or tape recorder and a recording of a symphony orchestra.

1. Play the recording of the orchestra for the children.

2. Ask them what instruments they can hear in the music.

3. Ask one child to pantomime playing one of the instruments they can hear.

4. Ask another child to join in playing another instrument.

5. Continue to add more children until you have just one child left.

6. Ask the last child to be the conductor.

7. Have the children pantomime to the music.

GROUP PANTOMIMES

Time: 15 Minutes.

Materials: Slips of paper with situations written on them.

1. Divide the children into groups of five or six.

2. Give each group a slip of paper with a situation on it.

3. Ask one group to come forward, and perform their situation for the other groups.

4. Have the groups guess the situation.

Some situations might be:

> A group of teenagers at a local malt shop
> A losing bowling team
> A circus tightrope act
> Passengers on an airplane that's about to crash
> Robots whose batteries are low
> Cheerleaders at a losing football game

IMPROVISATION SCENES

The ability to improvise on stage is a skill all actors need. No production is ever the same. There may be unexpected set problems, a difficult audience, a dropped line, or even a missed entrance. Actors must be ready to fill in the gaps. These simple exercises in improvisation will build up the confidence of young actors and actresses, and help them deal more effectively with the unexpected situations that occasionally arise on stage.

LET'S SING

Time: 20-30 minutes.

Materials: Words to two or three popular songs.

1. As each participant arrives, give them a line from a popular song.

2. When everyone has received a line from a song, instruct them to find other members of the group who have lines from the same song.

3. Once group members have found each other, they should put the lines together in the correct order.

4. Group members should practice singing the song, and then do a performance of their song for the entire group.

The leader must be certain that there are equal numbers of lines cut from each song so that one group is not larger than another.

KILLER

Time: 20 minutes.

Materials: None.

1. Ask all members of the group to close their eyes and put their thumb up in front of them.

2. Tell them that you will push one member's thumb down. This person will become the KILLER and is not to reveal his or her identity.

3. When the KILLER has been chosen, have group members wander around the room shaking hands with each other.

4. The murderer kills by using his or her index finger to lightly scratch the inside of the victim's palm.

5. When a group member is killed he or she should continue to walk about for a few moments before beginning the "big death scene."

6. The killings continue until someone discovers who the murderer is.

7. If someone accuses the another player of being the murderer, but is wrong, the accuser must die also.

8. Continue playing until everyone is dead or the murderer is discovered.

This is a good game to play with older children.

ON STAGE!

Time: 15-20 minutes.

Materials: None.

1. Give the group a topic, such as a dinner party, a high school reunion, a circus parade, or a shopping mall.

2. Ask the group to arrange themselves on stage as if they are at such an event.

3. At the count of three, have the group act out the topic. Then, when the command "freeze" is said, they should stop instantly and become a statue.

4. When they are frozen in their statue positions, the leader then tries to determine which members of the cast have their backs to the audience.

5. The cast members that are identified with having their backs to the audience are asked to sit down.

6. This continues until there are only a few members still on stage.

Participants must be constantly aware of the audience in this exercise.

BLANKETS

Time: 20-30 minutes.

Materials: One large blanket.

1. Begin by placing a large blanket on the floor in front of the group.

2. Explain that the blanket represents a swimming pool. Who can pretend they are swimming across? Allow several players to demonstrate, and then ask for suggestions as to what else the blanket can become. Ask players to pantomime their answers.

3. Ask one player to come forward and place the blanket around his or her shoulders like a cape. What could this player be: a king, a prince, superman?

4. Ask another player to come forward and do the same. Who could this player be? An Indian? Someone who is cold? Players should be encouraged to come up with other situations.

5. Next, have two players use the blanket, and mold it to become a horse, a tent, a cradle, and so forth.

6. As a group, use the blanket to create a merry-go-round, a hippopotamus, a slide, a fort, and whatever the imagination can create.

You may want to furnish several blankets and divide the group into teams. Have a creativity contest. Which group can think of the most situations?

THE CAR

Time: 15-20 minutes.

Materials: None.

1. Explain that as a group you are going to create a car.

2. Ask the players to tell you the parts of a car. Try to get them to really think about the different parts of a car.

3. Start with the engine. Ask players to make the sound of the engine. Choose one player to become the engine and position that player in front of the group.

4. Have the engine make an engine sound whenever you say "GO."

5. Next choose another part of the car—perhaps, the wheels. Ask four players to make the sounds and motions of the wheels. Position these players around the engine.

6. Continue to add the other parts of the car: lights, radio, doors, windshield wipers, horn, etc., until you have each member of the group playing some part of the car.

7. Always use the signal "GO" to get players to make their car sounds.

This same basic exercise can be used to construct any type of machine.

LET'S GO TO THE ZOO

Time: 15-20 minutes.

Materials: Some tables or chairs.

1. Select half of the group to become animals at the zoo.

2. Each player selected to be an animal must first pantomime for the group the animal chosen to be portrayed.

3. The animals take their places in their cages. (On tables or chairs throughout the room.)

4. The other half of the group becomes the people walking through the zoo.

Include a collection of funny animals such as monkeys and tortoises. Add some oddball visitors like an over eager photographer, a nasty little kid who pesters the animals, and a person who is terrified the lions will get loose. This is sure to be a fun experience.

GROUP PRETEND

Time: 20-25 minutes.

Materials: None.

1. In a large group, instruct players that you will call out the name of an object, and you would like them to form that object as soon as possible.

2. Call out a canoe. Wait a few minutes for the group to organize and form themselves into a canoe. If this does not happen, discuss that they will probably have to have a leader or two to help them work together. Appoint a leader and let them start again.

3. Call out several other objects and wait for the group to form them. Examples might be: a merry-go-round, a forest, a string a beads, and a giant tent.

4. After the group has mastered working together, divide them into two groups. The groups can race to see which team can organize

themselves the fastest into the following objects: a helicopter, a train, a sled, a cave, a house, and a playground.

Have the groups form an object and then try to guess what it is.

MACHINES

Time: 15-20 minutes.

Materials: None.

1. Tell the group that you want to build a machine that has never been invented.

2. Ask them to brainstorm for a type of machine that is needed but has never been built.

3. Discuss what parts would go into this machine.

4. Select one player to start. The player should select a specific sound and motion to make as though he or she were the base of the machine. This will be an action which is repeated over and over; for example, swinging his arms back and forth.

5. Add another player to begin an action that coordinates with the first. This player may choose to turn his or her body every time the first person's arms swing.

6. Gradually, add other players to the machine. Each player joins by making a different movement and sound.

7. When all players have joined the machine, you may want to put it on fast forward so that it explodes and all players fall to the ground.

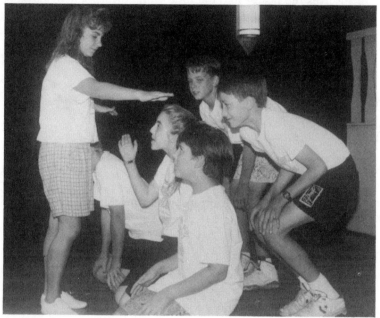

Machine making in improv class.

You may want to add a rule that no player can use a movement that is already being used. That way you'll be assured to get some unique actions.

MEETINGS AND GREETINGS

Time: 20-30 minutes.

Materials: None.

1. Instruct half of the group to line up on one side of the room and the other half on the other side of the room. They should face each other and be opposite a partner.

2. At the count of three, each group walks forward and greets their partner with a simple "hello." They then return to their original positions.

3. Next have the group greet their partners with an angry "hello" and return to their places.

4. These meetings continue with the "hello" expressed in different moods such as happy, scared, and embarrassed.

5. When the group is comfortable with the "hello" greeting, progress toward an improvised greeting of their own choice.

6. Have them improvise a greeting and a character as they meet their partner once again.

7. Continue with these meetings and greetings by varying the ways in which the partners walk toward each other and the emotions that they portray each time.

Keep a keen eye open for unusual greetings. Have these partners portray their characterizations for the whole class.

ADD ON STORIES

Time: **5-10 minutes.**

Materials: None.

1. Have the group sit in a circle.

2. One player begins telling any story that comes to mind.

3. After a minute or two, the player stops and the player to the right must continue the story.

4. The story progresses around the circle until the last player finishes it.

You may want to give the group a simple beginning to get the story moving. Some examples: It was a dark and dreary night out on my ranch . . . One rainy October day I . . . Last night I woke up and saw a . . .

CHAIN SENTENCE

Time: 5-10 minutes.

Materials: None.

1. Players sit in a circle.

2. One player begins a sentence by saying a single word.

3. The next player in line continues the sentence by adding a word.

4. This process continues around the circle with each player adding a word to keep the sentence going until it reaches a logical conclusion.

This exercise works best with a small group.

DIALOGUE DEVELOPMENT

One of the biggest problems for child performers is poor voice control. They speak too slow, too fast, too soft, or too loud. It is difficult for them to judge what type of voice is needed for an individual role. Even young actors need to learn to portray the character they are depicting through the use of their voice.

Learning to speak clearly and concisely on stage is a difficult task for children. They believe if they can hear each other then the audience must be able to hear them too. They need to work specifically on exercises that will help them speak slowly and precisely with more confidence. The following exercises reinforce pronunciation but at the same time will help build expression and projection skills.

Many of the activities included here will offer young performers the opportunity to experiment with a variety of expressions and emotions which will eventually help them with character development on stage.

VOCALIZING

Time: 5 Minutes.

Materials: None.

1. Ask the children to lie on their backs. They should place their hands below their rib cages.

2. Have the children repeat several sounds after you.

3. Examples of the sounds might be:

ha, ha, ha
he, he, he
ho, ho, ho
hi, hi, hi
hu, hu, hu
ooo, ooo, ooo
eee, eee, eee
be, be, be

NUMBER COUNTING

Time: 15-20 Minutes.

Materials: None.

1. Ask one child to come forward, and count to twenty in a loud voice.

2. Repeat this with several children.

3. After several children have been in front of the group counting, ask one child to count to twenty again in a loud voice but do it as if he or she is very angry.

4. Ask another child to count as though he or she is really happy.

5. Continue to ask children to count to twenty in various moods.

Examples of moods might be: scared, embarrassed, nervous, and excited.

Experimenting with emotions in dialogue exercises.

TWO-PERSON NUMBER COUNTING

Time: 15 -20 minutes.

Materials: None.

1. Ask two children to come forward.

2. Have them both count together up to twenty.

3. Ask them to count to twenty again; only this time one child says only the odd numbers and the other one only the even.

4. Repeat this with several different pairs.

5. Choose another pair and have them count to twenty once again; only this time they should do it as if they are having an argument.

6. Choose another pair and have them count to twenty as though they are very happy to see each other.

7. Repeat this exercise changing the moods each time.

NURSERY RHYME MEETINGS

Time: 15-20 minutes.

Materials: None.

1. Ask each child to think of a popular nursery rhyme.

2. Call on several children to recite their rhymes for the group.

3. Pick one child and ask him or her to stand in front of the group and recite the rhyme. Have the child repeat the rhyme until it can be recited easily.

4. Choose another child and have him or her say another rhyme in front of the group.

5. When you are certain both children know their nursery rhymes well, have them face each other and at the same time repeat their nursery rhymes as loud as they can.

6. You may want to vary this by adding moods to the rhymes. For example, one child can be angry and the other one happy.

NUMBERS

Time: 15-20 minutes.

Materials: Copies of nursery rhymes or short poems.

1. Distribute copies of nursery rhymes or short poems to the entire group.

2. Allow several minutes for the group to translate the poem into numbers. The number od digets used should match the syllables in each word, for example, Mary = 20, or had = 8. The phrase "Mary had a little lamb" might read "20-8-3-16-5."

3. Ask the players to recite the poems using only the numbers. They should be encouraged to add expression so that the meaning of the poem is illustrated using only the numbers.

EXPRESSION

Time: 5-10 minutes.

Materials: Blackboard and chalk.

1. Divide the group into pairs.

2. Write a sentence on the board and have each pair practice repeating the sentence in various expressions.

Some sample sentences are:

"Did you say no?"
"You can't mean that?"
"I can't go with you."

HOLD THY TONGUE!

Time: 2-3 minutes.

Materials: None.

1. Ask players to hold their tongues with their fingers, and then practice reciting the alphabet or counting to one hundred.

You can also have fun saying the alphabet in Spanish or French.

STORYTIME

Time: 15-20 minutes.

Materials: Children's storybooks.

1. Ask each player to select a familiar storybook to bring to class.

2. Take turns reading the books to the class.

3. Have them experiment with reading the books in a normal voice, a happy voice, a sad voice, and voices expressing other moods.

Dr. Seuss books work well for this exercise.

PARTNER SKITS

Time: 20-30 minutes.

Materials: Partner skit scripts.

1. Divide the group into pairs and give each pair one of the following short skits to perform.

2. They should be asked to perform the skit first using normal expressions and then again in various moods.

Skit 1
Player 1: You're early.
Player 2: I know.
Player 1: I'm glad.
Player 2: Me too.
Player 1: Can you stay long?
Player 2: Awhile.
Player 1: Shall we go?
Player 2: Alright.

Skit 2
Player 1: It's late.
Player 2: I know.
Player 1: Where were you?
Player 2: Around.
Player 1: Well, I can't stay.
Player 2: Me neither.
Player 1: See you.
Player 2: Goodbye.

Skit 3

Player 1: It's you.
Player 2: Didn't you expect me?
Player 1: Not really.
Player 2: Well, I'm here.
Player 1: Are you staying this time?
Player 2: Yes.
Player 1: Me too.
Player 2: Let's go.
Player 1: Alright.

Skit 4

Player 1: Hi!
Player 2: Oh, it's you!
Player 1: That's right!
Player 2: I knew you'd come.
Player 1: Did you?
Player 2: Yes.
Player 1: But I've got to go.
Player 2: Do you?
Player 1: Yes, goodbye.
Player 2: Goodbye.

Skit 5

Player 1: Oh, hello there.
Player 2: Hello, how are you today?
Player 1: I'm fine, and you?
Player 2: I'm just great!
Player 1: Terrific!
Player 2: Well, see you around.
Player 1: Sure, see you around.

Skit 6

Player 1: Late again?
Player 2: Sorry.

Player 1: Can you stay?
Player 2: No.
Player 1: Me neither.
Player 2: Then, this is goodbye.
Player 1: I'm afraid so.
Player 2: Goodbye, then.
Player 1: Goodbye.

Skit 7
Player 1: You're here?
Player 2: So are you!
Player 1: Can you stay?
Player 2: No, can you?
Player 1: No. Well, I better be going.
Player 2: Goodbye.
Player 1: Goodbye.

Skit 8
Player 1: Well, this is odd.
Player 2: Yes, seeing you here.
Player 1: I never expected you to come.
Player 2: I had to.
Player 1: Me too.
Player 2: But, I can't stay.
Player 1: Me neither.
Player 2: Goodbye.
Player 1: Goodbye.

PROJECTION

Time: 5-10 minutes.

Materials: None.

1. Divide the group into partners.

2. Partners should stand about a yard apart, facing each other.

3. One partner says a sentence, and then they each take a step back.

4. They continue with the partner saying the sentence, and each taking a step back—moving farther and farther away from each other.

5. See how long they can understand what the partner is saying without shouting.

Try this same exercise by whispering the sentence.

THE PRODUCTIONS

CHOOSING A PLAY

Once your company has the director and the children, you are ready to begin organizing a production. This may be in conjunction with your classes and that's fine. It is always better to begin once the children have already had a few classes under their belts and understand some of the basics of stage procedure.

In choosing your first play, set your sights low. Don't try to do a forty-member extravaganza for that first production. Choose a script that will help your cast members build their acting skills. But, always aim for quality. Don't pick a script that talks down to either the cast members or the audience. Children are very intelligent and intuitive. They know the difference between a simple kid's play and a real stage play. Unfortunately, most of the plays written for children are not respectful to children's acting skills. They portray children's characters in the simplest of terms. Look for a script that will challenge your young actors and actresses.

FINDING A SCRIPT

Finding quality children's scripts is a challenging job. There are a wide variety of play production companies, but not many of them carry plays that are realistic to perform with children. The best resources for suitable plays will be in catalogs which have a separate listing of children's plays, and the more plays the better. You want to deal with the companies that feel children's scripts are an important market and just don't carry a few stereotypical scripts.

The following companies will probably be your best source of quality scripts. See the appendix for addresses.

>   Players Press, Inc.
>   Samuel French, Inc.
>   Pioneer Drama Service
>   Clarus Music, Ltd.
>   Dramatic Publishing Company
>   Contemporary Drama Service
>   I. E. Clark, Inc.

WHO SHOULD CHOOSE THE SCRIPT?

If you are in sole directorship of your children's acting company, then you will want to be the one to select the script; however, it will take hours of reading to find the best one. It never hurts to have some help and suggestions on which is the best choice.

If you have eager parents and company members who like to read, ask them to be on a reading committee. They can save you hours of time by poring through the play catalogs, ordering scripts, and then previewing them before giving you suggestions of which ones look promising. Always try to have parents on the committee. Children are not very realistic when they are reading scripts. They don't visualize how much a script might cost to produce.

You may have to hurt their feelings when you veto a favorite story in favor of a less expensive one.

WHEN TO CHOOSE YOUR SCRIPT?

You should start to look for a script to produce at least five to six months before your production date. The first month you will be researching play catalogs looking for interesting titles. If this is your first production, plan on spending at least a hundred dollars on sample scripts. It will probably take two to three weeks for the scripts to be delivered, longer if you have to establish credit with the company. It will then take you approximately three to four weeks to read through the scripts before making a selection. You should have your final script decided on at least one month before you begin to audition your cast. This will give you time to advertise the auditions to your company. If you are teaching classes, it will give you time to read through the script in class so that the children know the story before auditioning.

WHAT TO CONSIDER WHEN CHOOSING A SCRIPT

Budget

The first consideration when ordering scripts is the amount of your budget. Most scripts will run about $4 each, so if you are ordering 25 scripts that is at least an investment of $100. Always check the royalty rates before selecting a script. If the title is a highly popular one such as *Tom Sawyer* or *Cinderella,* you will probably have to pay up to or over $50 per performance in royalty fees. Musicals like *The Wizard of Oz* can cost up to $200 in royalties per performance. The royalty fee can help you judge the popularity of a script. Be cautious of scripts that have a royalty of only $15.

These scripts are not as popular as others or the company wouldn't be charging such a low royalty rate. Look for a script that falls into the $25 to $50 range and you should have a good title.

Facility

Where you will stage your production is an important factor in script selection. You cannot stage a sixty person historical extravaganza in a school classroom. On the other hand, a four person single-set, one-act play would not be effective on a large stage. Choose a script that can be realistically staged on the performing area you have chosen. You must also take into consideration the special effects in the script. In the popular *Wizard of Oz* script produced by Tams Witmark, the play begins with a cyclone scene in which the cast exits through a trap door. If you do not have a trap door and cannot effectively stage this scene, don't plan on performing this script. Look for scripts that fit your needs; don't try to mold your performing area into something it isn't.

Type of Audience

Who will be attending your production? Will it be performed for a general audience of friends, relatives, and interested community members? Are you performing it for a school? Is it to be presented to an organization such as the Boy Scouts, Girl Scouts, or the 4-H Clubs? The type of audience that will be attending will dictate the type of script. If you know that there will be adults attending, you may want to choose a script that appeals to both adults and children. If only children are attending, you will want to stay away from scripts that feature hard-to-understand jokes or references that only adults would understand. Gear your script to the audience; if they are happy with your production, they will return.

Popularity of the Script or Subject

Scanning through play catalogs can become a tedious job. Many of the plays will be easily recognizable, such as *Raggedy Ann and*

Andy, Charlie and the Chocolate Factory, or *Annie.* Plays with these titles will win you an instant audience. Plays with titles such as *The Dancing Spider, I Didn't Know That,* or *Penny and the Magic Medallion* aren't very well known. Both groups of plays are wonderful to produce. They are fun for the audience and exciting for the cast. However, if you are just starting out, choose a "name" play. It will save you money and time in advertising your production.

Type of play

Choosing the style of play that you will present should be given careful thought. If you are working with a group that has little acting experience, you may want to choose a script which highlights the group instead of the individuals. Historical pageants, musical revues, or theme variety shows are excellent vehicles for beginning troupes. These types of shows allow children to work together to develop their skills with no pressure being placed on the individual. Fairytales are by far the most popular plays to do with children, but don't overlook the popularity of children's literature. There are some excellent adaptations in publication today of such classics as *Tom Sawyer, Heidi,* and *Charlotte's Web.* These are also excellent titles to do with an adult and child cast.

Size and Type of Cast

When you are choosing a script for your children's acting company, you will have one distinct advantage. That is, you should have a very good idea of how many characters you are looking to cast. If you have twenty-five children in your company, choose a script with twenty-five parts. Never choose a script with too many or too few parts. You can always double up on parts, but it is very difficult to add parts. By choosing a script with the exact number of parts you expect to cast, you are ensuring that everyone has a part. If some of the children get nervous or decide the time commitment is too heavy, you can always recruit another child, double up, or eliminate the part. If, on the other hand, some child does not get a part, no matter how big, you will be confronted by a tearful company member and an angry parent.

You should also take into consideration the types of children you will be casting. Do you have more girls or more boys? Do you have more older children or more younger children? Do you have several that are ready to carry large roles? Do you have several who may want to be onstage but aren't ready to speak onstage? Evaluate your group carefully and choose a script which highlights them rather than one that is too difficult and may end up embarrassing them.

READING THE SCRIPT

When you sit down with your sample scripts, the task of reading each from cover to cover may seem overwhelming, but it is a job that can often go quite quickly. If you know what you are looking for, you should be able to pinpoint a few scripts that have to be read carefully. The other scripts you can just skim through and set aside if they don't meet your criteria. I always suggest that potential directors check the following parts of a script carefully:

- cast list
- description of characters
- total number of scenes and pages
- period and setting of the play
- set needs
- special effects
- costume requirements
- prop list
- first two or three pages of dialogue

Once you have looked over these parts of a script carefully, you should have a good idea of whether the script is appropriate to your needs.

ADAPTING TO THE FACILITY

THE STAGE AREA

Once you have chosen your performing area and are ready to develop your set design for that first production, keep in mind the points in the following paragraphs.

You do not have to follow the set suggestions given in the script. Too often directors feel that the directions given in the script for set development must be followed exactly. These are only suggestions. You have no way of knowing what type of stage the play was originally staged on or even if it has ever been staged. Develop the set design to fit your individual space. It may mean that you will have to eliminate doors or even scenes, but if you design your set to complement your space, you will have a success.

Always design the simplest set possible. This does not necessarily mean that you have to compromise on quality. Some of the best sets built today are one-unit designs that use platforms on different levels to indicate different settings. The play *Tom Sawyer* calls for a variety of scenes including a church, a schoolyard, a graveyard, a street scene, and the interior of a church. A unit set that can encompass all scenes without ever changing flats or drops will eliminate a multitude of problems for your stagehands.

The sightlines of the audience should always be your first concern. No matter how clever your set design, if it blocks action from the audience it is a failure. Once you have designed your set, look for all possible obstacles to the audience's vision. Keep checking these sightlines as your set is constructed. Sit in different seats in the theater and check from all angles. Is there any piece of scenery that will be blocking someone's view? Don't assume that because you can see from the middle of the auditorium that everyone will be able to see.

Getting the stage ready for a play.

Add as much versatility as possible to your sets. Don't use the same exact set pieces to indicate two different scenes. If a scene is to take place at two different places in the forest, use one backdrop but with moveable trees to indicate different places. If you have two interior scenes but are using one set of flats, add pictures on the walls or different curtains on the windows. Don't assume that by merely turning the lights on and off the audience will realize you are changing scenes.

SAFETY FIRST

When you are ready to begin production on any play, one of the first things you should do is check out the safety of your performing facility. Whether your audience is ten people or a thousand people, you must meet certain legal requirements in order to have your facility licensed as a performing area. Foremost among these requirements is an adequate number of exits. You need to be sure that if there was an emergency your audience could exit quickly and efficiently. The number of exits required will vary in different states, but all are based on the seating capabilities of the theater. Check your local fire code on this matter.

Other items that must meet state and federal safety codes are: the number of restrooms, handicapped facilities, number and location of drinking fountains, the size of your aisle space, the dimensions between your rows of chairs, and the number of fire extinguishers on the premises. Ask a local building inspector to tour your facility with you and let you know areas that must be improved before your production. You will be very disappointed if the show must be postponed because it doesn't meet fire and building code regulations.

Even though your building may meet all of the required safety regulations, there are also a certain number of things that you should do to insure the safety of your cast. First of all, make sure that the building is located in a safe area. If you are going to have children coming and going from rehearsals and productions, you want to make sure that they can do so in relative safety. Are the hallways well lit? Is there a telephone for children who are not picked up on time to call their parents? Are there lights outside the building for the late night rehearsal times?

Do you have a first aid box handy at all times? You need to be prepared in advance for accidents. Anytime you have a group of active children together, there is bound to be some horseplay. Accidents are just the natural result of children rough-housing together. Scraped knees, bumped heads, stomped toes, and sprained ankles are just a few of the possibilities you may have to deal with during the course of a production.

Naturally, you will want to make your rehearsal/production area as accident free as possible. To do this you may want to do the following:

Secure Scenery and Props
When building a set, make certain that all platforms, boxes, moveable step units, flats, and heavy prop pieces are well anchored. Whenever possible, screw your set unit into the stage floor so that there is no possibility of it tipping or moving during the production.

Be Cautious During Set Changes
Rehearse slowly and carefully any set changes that must be made in the dark. If the children in your cast will be assisting in the set changes, make certain that they are well-prepared and aware of any obstacles they may meet once the lights are off.

Use Florescent Tape
Mark all set pieces with florescent tape to insure that no one stumbles into something dangerous.

Eliminate Sharp Objects
There should be no nails or sharp objects protruding from a set piece.

Be Careful with Cables and Cords
All cables and electrical cords should be secured to the floor with tape. Loose cables cause nothing but problems to cast members hurrying to make an entrance.

Keep Track of Props
Each prop piece not in use should be placed on a prop table and clearly marked. Never allow your cast members to throw their props down when coming offstage. Even the smallest prop dropped in the wrong place can cause a serious accident.

Keep Lighting on the Edge of the Stage
When working with children, the edges of the stage should be well lit at all times. Even during the course of a scene, children may

become excited and wander too close to the edge of a performing area.

Keep Flashlights Handy
Several flashlights should be kept backstage and be easily accessible to both the cast and crew. Stagehands should each carry a small flashlight.

Avoid Costumes That Restrict Vision
Children's costumes should be made so that the child can always see clearly. Never cover their faces with masks that obstruct their vision.

First Aid
Keep a fully equipped first aid box backstage.

Drinking Water
If there is no drinking fountain backstage, keep a jug of cold water and cups for cast and crew.

CASTING YOUNG ACTORS

WHO SHOULD CHOOSE THE CAST?

Casting a play of young people is a difficult job. There can be only one Alice in *Alice in Wonderland*, one Tom Sawyer in *Tom Sawyer*, and one Cinderella in *Cinderella*. If you are going to direct the play and cast it alone, be prepared for criticism. No one will be happy with your choices before the play. Everyone, parents and kids both, will have their own ideas on who should be playing who in the script. Be prepared for criticism. No matter how fair you are, someone will have their feelings hurt if they aren't selected for that "special" part. It is a director's responsibility to mold a play into a performance. Therefore, it is ultimately the director who must make the final decision in casting. However, you may want to have several people sit in on the auditions and give you their opinions on the selections. These people may include members of your acting company, parents, or even other professionals such as a musical director or choreographer.

PREAUDITION PREPARATIONS

The audition process can be stressful and lengthy if it isn't well planned. Before you begin, there are certain steps you should follow to make this experience as easy as possible for everyone involved.

Step One
Choose a room to hold your auditions in that will allow you to have some privacy. If you are holding auditions in the theater, then ask parents to wait outside. Children are often inhibited more by their own parents watching them than they are by a roomful of their peers. The room that you choose should be echo-free so that you can judge the voice tone of your potential cast members. If they are forced to yell during an audition in order to be heard, you are not really getting a true idea of their speaking ability.

Step Two
Prepare your company members in advance for the audition process. Discuss with the children who will be auditioning what will be expected of them. If you will be asking them to read from the script, supply sample pages for them to take home and study. Have them practice introducing themselves and answering a few questions about themselves. Help them understand the storyline of the play and the basic characters they will be auditioning to play.

Step Three
Choose several parts of the script that will be used for the audition. These parts should be ones that highlight the main characters. You can always cast the smaller parts from the same readings, but you should have a good idea of what your main characters can do on stage. You may want to type up a few selections from the script and have them enlarged so that the children can read the audition scripts easier. It is difficult to ask children to read cold from a regular-sized print script. You may unfairly judge a child's acting ability according to their reading ability. You can avoid this by making the reading process as easy as you can.

THE AUDITION

Generally, there are three parts to the audition process. You will start by asking the children to come forward and introduce themselves individually. At this time, the director will want to ask them a few questions. The questions do not really have to be for gathering information as much as for putting the young people at rest. Sample questions might be; What do you like to do in the summer? What's your favorite food and why? Who is your favorite friend and why do you like this person?

Once the children are relaxed in front of the director, they should be asked to read a short selection from the script. Before they begin, explain carefully what type of character you are looking for.

After a child has finished reading from the script, many directors will ask them to do some type of improvisation exercise. Although many children may seem stiff and uncomfortable with the reading section of an audition, most will relax and show off their acting abilities easier in an improvisation. It is always a good idea to suggest improvisations based on the story. For example, you are Snow White and you wandered into the three little bears' cottage by mistake, or you are Raggedy Ann meeting the greedy monster.

Choosing the best Tom Sawyer can be a struggle.

If the play is a musical, you will want the child to sing for the music director during the audition. If the songs in the script are not easily recognizable, then choose a song that the child is sure to know. "Happy Birthday," "Jingle Bells," and even "We Wish You a Merry Christmas" can give you a good idea of a child's voice quality.

AFTER THE AUDITION

There is only one way to notify your cast members that they have received the role. Telephone them each individually no matter how big your cast. Posting a list on your office door will only cause hard feelings. When you talk to each child individually you can convince them that they were the only possible choice to play their individual role. Even a child who has the nonspeaking role of the witch's cat will feel good about the role when the director explains that he or she was the only one who has that cat walk down. Speaking to the children individually insures that they will feel special and reduces the possibility of them feeling inadequate because they didn't get the big role.

Any time children are competing for something, whether it's a Little League position or a starring role in a play, there are bound to be complications when they don't accomplish what they set out to do. Generally, children can be convinced that any role in a play is important. Over the years, I have had more difficulty with meddling parents who were upset because their child didn't get the "big" part than I have had with the kids themselves.

If you encounter difficult parents, be patient. Often when a parent glares at you for weeks before the production, they will relax once the production is finished and their child receives praise for his or her "minor" role. Trying to justify or explain your casting choices is a poor decision. Keep in mind that you are the director and it is your responsibility to put together a successful show. Choose the children you feel will do the best job, and don't try to justify your choices!

REHEARSING WITH CHILDREN

You've chosen the play, found the location, cast the parts, and are ready to start rehearsing. Rehearsing a play with a cast of children is always a challenge. Kids enter into the spirit of theater with no holds barred. They are eager to "strut their stuff" and will try anything for a competent director.

There are two things you must beware of when rehearsing with children; one is, don't over-rehearse them, and the other is, don't under-rehearse them. Over-rehearsing tends to make the children stiff and robot-like on stage. Under-rehearsing will leave them unconfident and nervous. So how do you find the perfect medium? The answer to that question is to prepare a rehearsal schedule.

THE REHEARSAL SCHEDULE

Prepare a rehearsal schedule which evenly divides the time you will spend on each scene. Count backwards from your performance dates and determine how many total rehearsal sessions you will have. For a ninety-minute play, you will want to rehearse approximately thirty to forty hours. I've found that the perfect way to divide a script for child actors is to break the rehearsal time into half-hour sessions and plan on covering three to five pages per session. If you are going to rehearse for a total of four weeks before your opening night, then plan four to five two-hour sessions a week. During this two-hour time schedule, four separate three to five-page sections of the script will be covered. Try to alternate cast members' time so that only the main characters have to stay for the entire two-hour session.

Children are basically very busy people. In between schoolwork, piano lessons, Little League, and countless other activities, they will try to squeeze in play rehearsals. Don't make that task more difficult. Cut your rehearsal time to a minimum. If some children are not needed at rehearsal, let them stay home. Never have the whole cast at the rehearsal unless everyone will be in the scene you are working on. Asking children to sit around and watch others working will only create unnecessary problems. They will become bored and you will find yourself wasting precious rehearsal time disciplining children who don't even need to be at the rehearsal.

Remember also, that children are generally dependent on others to get them to and from rehearsals. Be understanding. It may not be feasible for a child to make every rehearsal. Mom or Dad may have business conflicts, or perhaps a family vacation was

Stagedoor players in rehearsal.

planned weeks before. Be flexible whenever possible. You may
have to reschedule, but in the long run your program will benefit.

THE FIRST REHEARSAL PERIOD

When you are rehearsing a play with an adult cast the first thing
you will do is sit down together as a cast and read through the
entire play. This doesn't work with children. Reading through an
entire play tends to bore the children and leave them frustrated.
Instead of reading the play as a group, require that they read
through it individually or with a parent before rehearsals begin.
Children are very moment oriented. They need to know that play
rehearsals will be fun. Sitting and reading a lengthy script isn't fun.
So, start to work right away.

Before you begin the actual rehearsal session, you may want to engage in some kind of a warm-up game or relaxation exercise. This is more important if the rehearsal time is right after a long school day. If the children have had time to go home and relax before coming to rehearsal, you may not have to do this.

Another thing you will want your cast to do before the first rehearsal is to go through the script on their own and highlight their parts in a bright color. This will help them with their memorization. Always have the children label their scripts with their own name. Through the years I've found that at least half of my cast will lose their script within the first two weeks of rehearsal. If the scripts are not labeled with cast names, you will spend the first fifteen minutes of every rehearsal time helping cast members find their script.

When working with either adults or children, a director should never keep the cast waiting. Always arrive at play rehearsals at least fifteen minutes before your cast. This will give you a chance to set up the stage. It will also give you a chance to greet cast members upon their arrival and answer any questions they may have formed since the last rehearsal session.

When you begin the actual rehearsal time, move very slowly. Sometimes I will only do half a page at a time until the children have completely memorized the words and blocking for that section. Once they have completed that half page to my satisfaction, I need only to brush up on it until the performance date.

Children are very fast learners, but you must proceed slowly. Never assume that a child will automatically do a particular movement. If the script calls for the child to walk diagonally across the stage, demonstrate for the child first. You may have to show them several times before they are able to copy the movement you want. But, once a child has mastered the particular movement and receives praise for it, they will almost always repeat it successfully. On the other hand, if you allow a child to do a movement wrong even one time, it will be a continual struggle to get the movement right.

BLOCKING THE PLAY

Blocking the play refers to the actual movement of the cast on stage. Who walks where, who stands where, who picks up what, and so forth throughout the play. Never lock yourself into what the script says to do. Script directions are merely suggestive actions. It is up to the director to determine all of the movements a cast will make throughout the course of the play. Block the play in a way that seems natural for both your young actors and your set design.

Position the children in a V-formation on stage so that each player is visible to the audience. One thing you will constantly have to remind children of when blocking a play is to keep their bodies turned toward the audience. Children want to see the action. They have a hard time relating to the fact that if they can see the main character the audience probably can't. They will constantly edge over and around toward the front of the stage to see the action better. Correct this from the very beginning of rehearsals. Teach the V-formation early on in rehearsals and use a signal to remind children to turn their backs in the right direction.

While blocking a play, keep in mind that children are very creative. You may want to wait until rehearsal to work out some of the stage direction with the cast. During a production of *Wizard of Oz*, I was frantically trying to pull the curtain call together at the last rehearsal. I was tired and feeling very uncreative. The child who played the Scarecrow came out on stage for his final bow and characteristically staged a great fall. Of course, the rest of the cast giggled, and from there we added all kinds of wonderful movements to the end of the play. Children can be very helpful in the blocking process. Ask for their input as you proceed through the course of the script.

You will have more success with blocking the play if the children do not have the play books in their hands. Encourage them to memorize their lines before you begin to block.

MEMORIZING LINES

Even the littlest actors and actresses (five and six years old) can memorize lines if they are taught a few easy ways to do it. Of course, reading through the script everyday and practicing a few times a day with an adult is the best way. One of my little cast members always came to rehearsal excited about the lines he would have to memorize for the next day. When I questioned him, I discovered that his mother had set up special McDonald's breakfasts with him so that they might have time to memorize the lines he would need to know at the next rehearsal. Naturally, he was anxious to have more lines to memorize—it meant a special time alone with his mother.

I always encourage parents to become involved in helping the childern learn their lines. However, that may not always be possible. Another solution for memorizing lines is for the children to record the play on a tape recorder. The children should read aloud all the lines in the play in order except their own lines. They should skip their own lines and leave space on the tape. Then, they can replay the tape and practice saying their lines where they are located in the play.

Another way for children to memorize the play comes in the directing process. If you are only covering two to three pages at each rehearsal time, the child should be able to memorize lines during the course of the rehearsal. Just repeat the lines a paragraph at a time while you practice them on stage. You'll find that if you use this method the child will have mastered the lines by the end of the rehearsal period.

It is important to stress with children that saying the exact line in the play is not as important as keeping the storyline intact. They may miss a line, but if they can keep the play moving and even add in a comparable ad-lib, no one will even notice the mistake. I always stress the story while I am directing. I take time to explain why the witch would say something nasty to Snow White at that time or why Aunt Polly might be angry with Tom during this particular moment. If children understand the scene, they can keep the action moving.

One time I had an intern director take over a short production of *The Brementown Musicians* for me. During an actual performance a child missed a major line. None of the children could cover the mistake. When I talked to the children afterward I discovered that they didn't understand the story; therefore, they didn't know what was happening, so they couldn't decide what the characters would say during that scene. Teaching the storyline is more important than teaching the dialogue. Children can be masters at ad-lib, but they have to understand the situation first.

DRESS REHEARSAL

Dress rehearsals are always a confusing experience whether you have a cast of adults or a cast of children. Plan on that! Never schedule only one dress rehearsal. Plan on the first dress rehearsal being complete pandemonium. Then, your second dress rehearsal should give you the finished product. At the first dress rehearsal children will be complaining about their costumes, teasing other people, and overall just getting used to working in costume. Allow them to do this. Expecting children to pull off a perfect dress rehearsal on the first try is unrealistic.

Try not to stop the action during a dress rehearsal no matter how badly the cast is doing. Don't shout directions, cue lines or help in any way. The director needs to be invisible. A dress rehearsal is the time for a cast to show the director what the play will look like for the audience. But, it is not a time for the director to simply relax. Keep a clipboard handy and write like crazy. Write down every comment you can think of that will help improve the quality of the play. Whenever possible, write comments about individual cast members.

Preparing for the dress rehearsal.

At the end of the dress rehearsal, don't try to discuss your notes with the cast; instead, give them a few overall comments and allow them to go home. Before they return for the next dress rehearsal or even for the actual performance, post a copy of your notes in several places backstage. Then twenty to thirty minutes before you begin the performance, discuss the notes with the cast. Children absorb things better if they can see it written down on paper. Before a performance they are too nervous to remember something they are told. If they have time to read it, they will remember.

VIDEOTAPING A REHEARSAL

Many directors videotape rehearsals and then review them with the
cast. I've found that this only creates problems with children.
Don't let children see their own performance until the production
is finished. Seeing themselves on film tends to inhibit children.
Children have wonderful imaginations. If they are using their
imaginations to create the character of Raggedy Ann, they might
be shocked when they see themselves actually acting the role.
Although they may seem quite successful in the role to the
audience, seeing themselves on film may not be what they had
imagined. Viewing videotapes of ourselves is always something of

Players dressed for *Tumbleweeds*.

a shock. We all like to believe that we don't have a little rasp to our voice or perhaps aren't taller than someone else. When we see proof on film, it can ebb our self-confidence. Avoid problems by keeping video cameras out of rehearsals.

SET DESIGN AND CONSTRUCTION

When designing the set for your production keep in mind that a set is much more than just the scenery. The style, color, and tone of the set, along with the props and even the costumes, all add to the total picture the audience will see.

TYPES OF STAGES

As I stated earlier in the book, a production does not have to be staged in an auditorium to be theater. You may choose to stage your production in a church hall, a civic center basement, a gymnasium, or even a classroom. However, before you choose your facility you should be familiar with the different types of stages. Basically, theater happens in four different kinds of areas: the theater-in-the-round, the thrust stage, the proscenium stage, and the black box theater. I've included here a brief description of each type of theater as well as a floor plan diagram.

Theater-in-the-Round
Theater-in-the-round dates back to the time of the early Greeks, when audiences sat on the hillsides surrounding the players. During the 1960s, there was a revival in this country of theater-in-the-round performing complexes. This type of performing area can be recreated quite easily. You will only need a large room with

several different entrances. An entrance at each of the four corners of the room is the ideal. You can create this type of theater by placing a large square platform in the middle of the room and surrounding it with your audience.

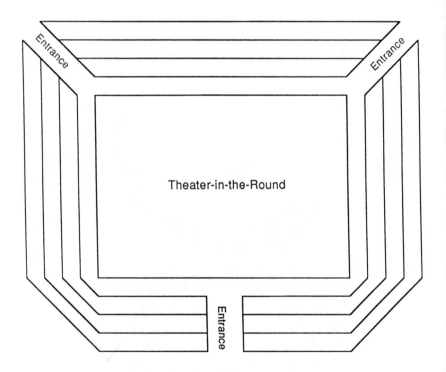

Theater-in-the-Round

Thrust Stage
The thrust stage dates back to the early Renaissance period. In a theater with a thrust stage, the audience surrounds the stage on three sides. This has advantages over theater-in-the-round because the back wall may be used for scenery.

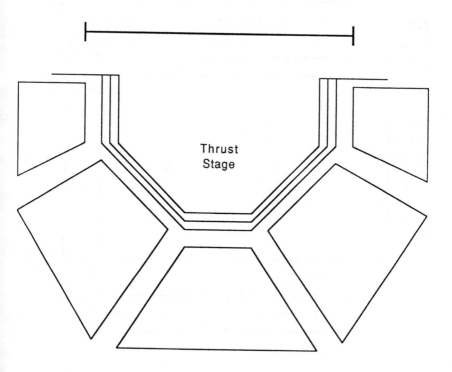

Thrust
Stage

Proscenium Stage

The proscenium stage came to being during the Victorian Era in England when theater was seen to be an elite experience. Audiences viewing a play on a proscenium stage are somewhat removed from the action by the proscenium arch which extends across the front of the stage defining the acting area.

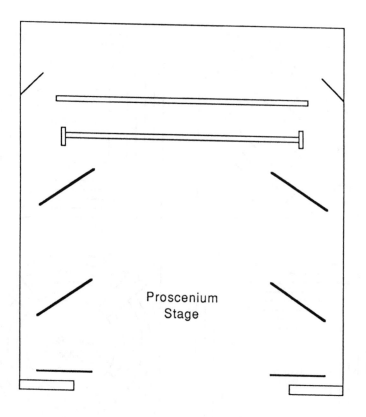

Proscenium
Stage

Audience

Black Box Theater
A popular theater that has sprung up in universities across the nation is the black box theater. This is nothing more than a big room. The set designer for a black box theater has the ultimate in versatility. With the help of a set of moveable rostras, the set designer may choose to design each set at a different point in the room.

All four of these types of performing areas can stage successful productions, but it is up to the set designer to determine what will work most effectively in the performing area chosen.

RESEARCHING THE PLAY

Whenever I begin to design a set, I always spend a few hours researching the story. My first step is a visit to our local library where I spend some time in the children's section. If the play I am producing is a popular fairytale, I never have any trouble finding colorful picture books that illustrate ideas for a set. If the play is not a well-known story, I've still found that the library can give me countless ideas for set design. During one year I had to design sets for the following plays: *Tom Sawyer, Seven Wives for Dracula, The Wizard of Oz, The Dancing Spider,* and *Peace Child.* All of these plays had drastically different sets, and I found ideas for all of them at the library.

Let me explain the research process on just one of these plays, *The Dancing Spider.* This play, published by Dramatic Publishing, is the story of Anansi the Spider. It is a popular South African folktale. I began my research by looking for Anansi books in the library. I was able to find several. One of the books used colorful abstract lines in the illustrations. I put this book aside.

I continued my research by looking for books on South Africa. I was able to find several that had color photographs of South African children dressed in their native costumes. I put these books aside also.

Next, I looked for folktale books. I was able to find a book that not only had another Anansi story but also contained a whole section on African Folktales and gave a short history on how these stories would be told around the village campfire with the use of large colorful puppets.

After I had exhausted the book section, I visited the periodical section for children. There, I was able to find several colorful magazines that illustrated African dress.

I brought these materials home to complete my research. From the books I had gathered, I was able to come up with a rather unique idea. The story is about a group of animals and takes place in the jungle. I decided to eliminate a traditional jungle scene and use large platforms instead. This gave me some versatility of entrances and exits on stage. Then, I copied the bright colors I had found in the Anansi book and painted my backdrop and platforms in vivid pinks and yellows. Next, I had my costume people copy the bright dress I had seen in the magazines. Instead of traditional animal costumes, we put each of the children in a native looking gown. Then, we added bright colored masks to represent the animals. The effect was very South African looking as you can see in the photo below.

The set to *The Dancing Spider.*

In my research I had discovered that the South African folktales were often illustrated using large puppets. Because the play *The Dancing Spider* was quite short, I decided to extend our performance by adding a second half. After a short intermission, our cast demonstrated several camp fire-type African dances while we used a narrator and puppets to tell another story of Anansi the Spider.

The puppets were quite easy to make from paper mache. They were an instant hit and the extended performance pleased everyone.

SETTING UP

Setting up the stage is an exciting day. You may want to allow some of the children in to help. I always make it a rule that a child working on the set must be accompanied by a parent. Not only does this give me adequate adult help but it also eliminates my supervision problems. Set construction can be hazardous. You will have electrical tools, nails, saws, and other dangerous items lying around that can cause injuries. You will need as much adult supervision as possible.

Throughout the entire set construction, you should be continually checking sightlines. Although a model may seem effective once it is constructed in a large scale, on stage you may find that it blocks the view for a small section of the audience.

Once your set is up, you will want to have several technical rehearsals so that your stage crew can perfect their movements in between acts. Take your time and walk through each set change that takes place. Spending the time to rehearse set changes without the cast present will guarantee a smooth production.

COSTUMING FOR KIDS

Many children's theater books will give you clever ideas for constructing inexpensive costumes out of paper and cardboard. While this may save you money initially, paper or cardboard costumes look like paper and cardboard costumes. If you want to look professional and gain a reputation as a professional troupe, then start with your costuming. Never allow your young actors and actresses to appear onstage in a costume that would not be suitable for an adult performer. I've visited hundreds of professional theater companies around the country and I have never seen a professional performer appear onstage in a paper costume. It is just not done and it shouldn't be done in professional children's plays.

Costumes are a very important part of your production. Often they help to introduce the character before any lines are spoken. When a young girl comes out on the stage dressed in a bright red dress with a matching hood, the audience can instantly recognize her as Red Riding Hood. Use your costuming to help your young actors get their characterization across. It is much more difficult to be playing the part of Red Riding Hood when you are wearing regular clothing with a crepe paper red apron than it is to play Red Riding Hood dressed in a real red dress and hood.

One of the most exciting parts of being in a play is wearing a costume. Children love wearing costumes; they love putting on a disguise that transforms them into another character and allows them, for a brief time, to escape their own personality and become someone else. Acting is like Halloween every day.

I've found that most of the children I cast in plays spend a lot of time in their costumes outside of rehearsals. One mother told me her son wanted to put on his costume every morning at nine o'clock even though the performances weren't until seven at night. I encourage them to do this. The more time they spend in their costume, the more time they will spend thinking about their role in the play. It is a good practice. Spending time in their costumes allows them to get a feel for the play and their part. But, if you are to encourage your young performers to spend time in their costumes you must make sure that they are issued a good costume.

WHAT MAKES A GOOD STAGE COSTUME?

First of all, a good stage costume must be durable. Children will toss hats in the air, twist aprons over their head, chew on gloves, crawl around on tights, and do everything a good detergent ad warns us about. Be prepared for the worst. Don't expect that children will take good care of their costumes. Backstage you will find them in heaps on the floor, crammed under shelves, or stuffed into backpacks. A good costume must be able to take all the abuse children can deal out.

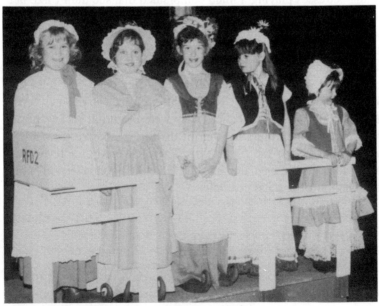

Costuming is an important part of the production.

A good stage costume must also be comfortable for the children to wear. Child performers are very easily distracted. Be certain that a child's costume does not add to their distraction. Loose buttons, belts that come unbuckled, tight shoes, and skirts that aren't tight enough will all cause a child to forget their lines and movements on stage. Provide the children with costumes that are easy to wear and also easy to forget about.

Another important thing to remember when costuming a children's play is the child's opinion of their costume. Several years ago for a performance of *Snow White*, I needed six maids-in-waiting costumes. In an attempt to save money, I decided to listen to one of the mothers who suggested that we cut down several old adult prom dresses that we had in our costume room. It seemed like a good idea at the time. The dresses had been donated several months before and had been hanging unused ever since. The girls were measured, the dresses cut down and that was the last I thought of it until the day before dress rehearsal when one of the young actresses playing a maid complained that she didn't like her costume. I asked her to model it for me thinking that all she needed was a little attention and she could be persuaded into liking it. However, when I saw the dress on her I realized it looked like an old prom dress cut down. She didn't feel like the character of a lady-in-waiting because she didn't look like one. She felt silly because she looked silly. That night, we made brand new costumes for each of the six ladies. They were beautiful. As I watched the girls twirling around in front of the mirrors before the show I knew we had done the right thing. They felt pretty, more importantly, their costumes made them feel like their characters. That is the function of a stage costume.

FINDING THE COSTUMES

If you are lucky enough to have a comprehensive costume room, you may have to go no further to find costumes for your produc-

Well-designed
costumes enhance
the performance.

tions. After more than ten years in children's theater, there are few costumes that I need to search for anymore. I have bears, rabbits, dogs, even a donkey in stock. You may not be so lucky. Remember, it has taken me ten years to build up my stockpile of costumes. If you do not have a costume room, your first resource for costumes should be the kids themselves. Always announce and send home a note of costume needs before you start to make any costumes. I average at least 25 percent of my costumes from relatives and friends of the cast. Every child in America has at least one old Halloween costume hanging in an attic or basement closet. All you need to do is put out the call. I am always amazed at the gorgeous costumes that once belonged to "my cousin George" who had to wear it for his school play or to "the neighbor child" who was in the church pageant.

Once you have collected all of the costumes you can from the cast, you will have to turn to other resources. Before you drag out the sewing machine and start searching through pattern books, check out a few other costume resources. Goodwill stores and other organizations that carry second-hand clothing are a great place to look. Garage sales also can be a wonderful way to find costumes. One Saturday morning spent searching at local sales can save you hours of sewing and lots of money. Use your imagination. What may look like a lady's old silk blouse may be the perfect tunic for the Prince in *Snow White*. Those old overalls that are being discarded at the garage sale next door may be perfect for *Tom Sawyer* to wear while he is painting the fence.

Once you have collected everything you can, you will probably still have to have a few costumes made. This can be very expensive. Avoid going to a professional seamstress. Once again, put out the call to parents. I've had several parents who wanted to be involved but, because of small children, couldn't volunteer to usher or help during the performances. Sewing costumes was a perfect way to use their time. It is something they could do at home and still feel involved. Never hesitate to ask. All they can do is say no.

COSTUME FEES

When my daughter was a little girl, she was enrolled in dance class for a few months. During this time, the class recital rolled around. I was appalled by the price I was expected to pay for a costume. She danced in one number and the costume price was over fifty dollars. I think that was when I determined never to charge my students more than ten dollars for a costume fee.

Obviously, many of the costumes you will use in a production will cost more than ten dollars. But, on the same note, many of the costumes will be less than ten dollars. By charging a straight ten dollar fee for costumes, I can pay for all the costumes and no one has to pay an exorbitant fee. It all evens out as the children participate in more plays. While they may not have a costly

Players model their wordrobes for *Raggedy Ann and Andy*.

costume in one play, in the next play they may have the most expensive one. I've found this system makes everyone happy, including me, since I get to keep all the costumes and build up my costume supply. There will, however, always be the child who wants to keep a costume. This generally happens with the new costumes that we have made specifically for a performance. I think that it is important for children to keep their costumes if they want to; for this reason I always offer them the chance to purchase their costumes after a performance. However, the purchase price runs the full price of the costume and can range anywhere from twenty to forty dollars depending on the costume.

RENTAL COSTUMES

I never encourage renting costumes. First of all, it is extremely expensive. A rental costume can run between $50 to $200 per week. Also, only a few costume companies rent to children, so it can be a frustrating experience just trying to find a rental company. Once you do find one, you will probably have to deal with delivery. If the company is not in your town, you will have to pay shipping costs, which can add up quite quickly. Then, you will be responsible for shipping the costume back on time. After a production, the last thing I want to worry about is returning costumes. Also, if you rent costumes you will never build up your own supply. It is always better to make or find your own instead of relying on a rental company.

ADVERTISING AND TICKET SALES

Directors new to the theater often think that if they stage a production successfully—that is, if the actors are convincing, the set, costumes, props are realistic, and the overall effect is entertaining—that the audiences will come. This is far from the truth. The audiences will come for only one reason—if it is advertised successfully. They will return to subsequent performances and bring their friends if the production is entertaining. This is an important factor to keep in mind. First, you advertise to get your audience; then, you prove to the audience that you will provide them with an entertaining production. You cannot reverse the order. If you do not have an audience, there will be no one to judge your production and spread the word to come to future productions.

So how do you begin to advertise? First, you must have a clear idea of what information you need to advertise. Basically there are six pieces of information that need to be given to the public. They are:

1. Who you are. This includes your theater company's name and logo.
2. What you are selling. The name of the play.
3. Where it is happening. The location of the performance. Be sure to include specific directions even if it is in a well-known place. There may be people from out of town who are not familiar with it.
4. When it is happening. The exact dates and times of performances.
5. Ticket prices. Be specific on prices for adults and children.
6. How to buy tickets. Where and when they are available.

Once you have gathered your information you are ready to begin your advertising campaign.

TARGET YOUR AUDIENCE

Start the process by first targeting who your audience will be. Make a list of potential customers. Who are they? First of all, there are the obvious: the relatives of the cast, parents, brothers and sisters, aunts, uncles, grandparents, and even young cousins—all eager to come and see the star in the family. Next look to the friends of your cast. Teachers, schoolmates, and neighborhood friends will all be susceptible to seeing a production featuring someone they know. After you have exhausted personal acquaintances, then ask yourself who else in the community would be interested in a children's production. How about schools, day-care facilities, families with young children, or even senior citizen centers? These all have potential customers.

TYPES OF PUBLICITY

Once you have chosen your audience, how do you reach them? There are many different ways. Posters, newspaper advertising, billboards, handbills, and displays in store windows can all be successful advertising methods. Use them all.

Posters
Posters can be placed in or on store windows, doctors' offices, company lounges, school corridors, church bulletin boards, grocery store counters, or any place that people congregate. They are a great way to advertise if they are done correctly. The success lies in the design of the poster.

Using the information you gathered earlier, design a poster that will appeal to potential customers. Keep it as simple as possible, but make sure that you have included all of the necessary facts about your production. You will also want to include some kind of an illustration. If you cannot find an artist to design some original art work, you may want to use the cover of the script. Art ideas for posters can be found on most playbook covers and can be used without charge just by purchasing the script. This is the best type of poster art to use since it is designed by professional artists.

Always have the posters printed by a professional company. If you only post posters that the children have made themselves, you are giving the public the wrong impression of your goal. If you want to become known as a professional company, look professional from your first contact with the public.

Handbills
Once you have decided on a poster design, you can then use the same design for handbills which can be distributed almost anywhere. I've always had good luck in asking elementary school principals to allow me to send handbills home with the school children. If your school is receptive to this idea, make sure that you help the school secretary out with the distribution of the handbills to classroom teachers. Ask how many handbills each classroom teacher will need and then deliver them to the school grouped together in the correct count needed for each teacher. You may want to deliver them to the classrooms yourself. This will also give you a chance to talk to the teachers and tell them a little about your program. Another popular use for handbills is to place them on the ends of local grocery store counters. Busy mothers will almost always pick one up at the end of their shopping.

Newspaper Ads
An expensive but successful way to let the public know about your performance is to place an advertisement in your local paper. Before you do this, ask the newspaper about rates and be very specific about the size of ad you want. Most advertising departments will try to talk you into a bigger ad than you actually need. All you really need to do is to get the information across about your performance. You don't need a half page ad to do that. You may also want to suggest to your local editor that, since you are a paying advertiser, he may want to do a story on your production. Most editors are receptive to this idea and, along with your ad, a story will help ticket sales.

News Columns
Most cities and small towns have a "what's happening" column which describes local events and activities. Listing in these

Advertise your program wherever you can.

columns is free of charge. Send a news release to all publications in your area briefly describing your production including the title, place, time, cost, and anything else about the cast or production that would be of interest to the local community. In order to serve their readers, editors frequently write articles on interesting local events. Like the "what's happening" columns, these news stories are free. An excellent book written on news releases and how to get free publicity is *Writing Effective News Releases: How to Get Free Publicity for Yourself, Your Business, or Your Organization* by Catherine McIntyre. This books covers all types of business including theater and performing arts, and provides many actual examples of releases that have proven successful.

Cast Sales
The best type of advertising you can get is word of mouth. I always ask each of the kids in my cast to try to sell at least ten

tickets. We have even had cast contests to see who could sell the most tickets. This pays off in several different ways. First of all, the kids have fun selling tickets, you benefit from the income generated by the tickets, and the kids in the cast benefit from having people in the audience that they know personally. Also, if you have 30 players in your cast and they sell ten tickets apiece, that is three hundred tickets. No advertising can guarantee that kind of success.

Other Types of Advertisements
When you are trying to market a production, try anything. I've had children walking up and down main street wearing costumes from the play. We've presented parts of the play at the library story hour. We've ridden in parades in costume. Anything that will tell the public who you are and what you are doing will help ticket sales.

COMMUNITY INVOLVEMENT

Community involvement is vital to any theater program. You will always need an audience and that audience will come from the community. You will also need help promoting your plays and that promotion comes ultimately from community members who support your program. Once you have won over your community, you have ensured yourself of a successful business.

In beginning to build up community involvement in your program you must be seen. Volunteer your group to perform for local audiences free of charge. The local Kiwanis, Jaycees, and Lion's Clubs are always looking for entertainment for their meetings. The local Chamber of Commerce looks for groups to perform at community events. Volunteer as much as possible, especially during your first few years. The more you are seen and liked, the more rapidly news of your theater program will spread.

During the past few years my kids have performed repeatedly for community functions. They enjoy the notoriety and the community enjoys the entertainment. Some areas we have performed at include the following.

Local Library
Librarians are always looking for something unusual to celebrate story hour.

Community Celebrations
Does your community have an annual celebration? You can volunteer to perform for free. March in the parade. Get your name before the public as much as possible.

School Programs
Teachers will be more than eager to have your group perform.

Church Celebrations
We perform regularly for the annual mother-daughter banquets at several local churches.

Civic Organizations
The Jaycees, Lion's Club, Kiwanis, or other community service organizations generally meet once a month. Volunteer to perform at one of their meetings.

Shopping Malls
Shopping mall directors are always looking for entertainment to get publicity and attract customers.

Hospitals
Large children's hospitals welcome any group that wants to entertain.

Homes for the Elderly
Volunteer to stage a Christmas show or Easter celebration for the local seniors.

Sample Advertising

Presents

The
Wizard of Oz

Produced by arrangement with
Tams-Witmark Music Library, Inc.

Performing at
STAGEDOOR CENTER
(Formerly the Gem Theater)

Fri.	April 5	7:30 p.m.	Thur.	April 11	7:30 p.m.
Sat.	April 6	2 p.m.	Sat.	April 13	7:30 p.m.
		7:30 p.m.			
Sun.	April 7	2:00 p.m.	Sun.	April 14	2:00 p.m.

Tickets $4.00
Reserved Seating
Tickets now on sale at Stagedoor Center
Call 715-246-4295

31-32Rc

the **STAGE DOOR PLAYERS** Present
Live Theater
for the
Whole
Family!

**Season Tickets Now
On Sale!**

Call the Box Office for a
Gold Star Membership
Brochure.

51ppc

Stagedoor Center
116 S. Knowles Ave. New Richmond
Box Office: 246-4295
Mon. - Fri. 10-5, Sat. 10-1

the **STAGE DOOR PLAYERS** Present

'Johnny
Appleseed'

Performed by The Stagedoor Adult
Professional Acting Company

Saturday, Sept. 14 .... 11:00 a.m & 2:00 p.m.
Sunday, Sept. 15 .... 2:00 p.m.
Saturday, Sept. 21 .... 11:00 a.m & 2:00 p.m.
Sunday, Sept. 22 .... 2:00 p.m.

Season Tickets
Now on Sale!

Reserved Seating · Tickets: $7.00

Stagedoor Center
116 South Knowles Ave. New Richmond, WI 54017
Box Office: 246-4295 · Mon. - Fri. 10-5, Sat. 10-1

4c

---

the **STAGE DOOR PLAYERS**

Present

A
Stagedoor
Showcase

featuring
A mini-musical & lively
demonstration of our
acting program.

**Thursday, May 16
Friday, May 17
7 p.m.**

Tickets $3.00

At Stagedoor Center

Box Office

246-4295
Mon.-Sat. 10-5

38c

THE BUSINESS

STARTING A BUSINESS

The one single factor that will make your children's theater group achieve the label of "professional" is when you begin to look on it as a business and not a hobby. To do that, you must establish yourself as a business person. Stop giving away your skills and start charging customers for your expertise in the area of children's drama. In the preceding chapters, we have covered how to form your group, how to organize classes, and how to stage productions. Now, we will discuss how to become established as a business.

FOR-PROFIT VERSUS NONPROFIT THEATER GROUPS

The majority of theater groups in this country are established on a nonprofit basis. This means that they rely primarily on volunteers for their labor, and they obtain donations and grants from individuals and corporations for their primary sources of revenue. They are run by a board of directors which is an appointed or elected group of people, none of whom earn their living from the theater. Directors, stage managers, producers, and often the actors and actresses are hired by the board and can be fired by the board. Establishing a theater independently as a for-profit, sole ownership business eliminates the need for a board of directors. However, both types of theaters have their advantages and disadvantages.

Nonprofit Theater Company

<u>Advantages</u>
Volunteer labor is generally in abundance.
Grants and monies can often be obtained from arts organizations.
No one person is responsible for all the decision making.

<u>Disadvantages</u>
Paid positions are rare.
Lengthy paperwork must be completed to obtain funding.
Disagreements or personality conflicts among the board can cause complications.

For-Profit Theater Company

<u>Advantages</u>
More artistic freedom to produce productions.
Sole decision making, the owner does not have to answer to anyone.
The profit from productions pays the owner a salary.

<u>Disadvantages</u>
The hours of commitment will be very long in the beginning years.
Volunteer labor will be limited.
Financial donations will be nonexistent.

For the remainder of this chapter we will be discussing how to

Teaching classes will be an important part of your business.

establish a for-profit theater company. Many of the same steps can be followed when establishing a nonprofit company.

TAKING A RISK

Establishing any business in today's world can be a risk to the potential owners, even if the business is a venture that has proven financially successful in other cities. Every town has restaurants, shoe stores, gift shops, and even dance studios that have proven successful. However, few towns across the nation have successful children's acting companies operated by a sole owner. So can it

be done? I did it and so can you, but there is a lot more to running
a successful business than simply choosing a name and location.

If you are establishing a children's theater company as your
own individual business, if you expect to someday make a living
off of the profits of your business, then you must follow certain
organizational guidelines in getting started.

First, examine your market. Is your town big enough to
support a children's theater? New Richmond, Wisconsin, where
my children's theater is located, has a population of under six
thousand. I still manage to have over two hundred children
enrolled in my program. However, I must draw from surrounding
communities for my ticket sales. No town of six thousand will
support more than two or three children's productions a year. If
you have a company of two hundred young actors, you will have
to perform a minimum of five productions a year.

Acting provides an excellent out-of-school activity for kids.

Next, take a look at your competition. If the local public elementary or middle school has a highly active successful drama program, your chances are going to be limited when it comes to getting parents to pay a tuition for enrollment in your program. Why should they pay for something their child can get free at school? Is there a local dance studio or gymnastics studio in your town that is highly successful? If so, it will be difficult to draw students away. Parents will generally only pay for one out-of-school activity for their children. I started my program at the same time a popular dance teacher in town opened her studio. We are both still in business, but her business peaked long before mine. Acting studios are not as socially acceptable as dance studios.

Another thing you will want to evaluate before going into business for yourself is your own personality. Ask yourself the following questions:

- Am I a self-starter?
- Am I a problem solver?
- Do I have good management skills?
- Am I a patient person?
- Am I a creative person?
- Do I enjoy working with lots of different people?
- Can I make decisions quickly?
- Is my personal life stable?
- Am I financially able to afford starting my own business?

If you can answer yes to these questions, you are probably ready to start your own business.

LEGAL REQUIREMENTS

As a new business owner, you will encounter a multitude of legal restrictions and requirements that you never knew existed. You will encounter restrictions from the moment you begin looking for a place to hold classes and stage productions. Do a thorough investigation of the zoning laws in your community. Zoning regulations will explain which activities are permitted and which are prohibited in certain parts of a city or county. Call your local city hall or zoning office to get a copy of the local zoning laws.

Most towns will have registration and licensing requirements which you must meet; however, since children's acting companies are not too common, most city officials will be perplexed when it comes to determining what category your business comes under. You should receive the same type of licensing that an independent dance or gymnastic studio receives. A license is a permit to practice a certain business activity. It is issued by either the local, state, or federal government, depending on your location. When you register your acting company as a business, you will also receive a sales tax number. Businesses that do not follow necessary legal steps when starting can be just as quickly closed down. Don't take the risk!

THE BUSINESS PLAN

When my accountant first suggested developing a business plan, I had to suppress my laughter. I wasn't thinking of opening a multimillion dollar business. I just wanted to teach some acting classes and put on a few plays with kids. The whole idea of a business plan seemed ridiculous. Now that I own my own building and have several full-time employees, I realize that it was my beginning business plan that helped me establish a credible business.

A well-written business plan provides the potential business owner with documented goals for the business. It is somewhat like a road map showing your destinations. It will prove invaluable when you are applying for funding and will help you develop and maintain your managerial skills. Taking the time to complete your business plan will also enable you to evaluate more fully whether developing a children's theater company is a viable option for you to pursue.

A business plan includes the following items.

Historical Information on Your Company
This explains your expertise in the area and documents your major successes and achievements.

Business Development
In this area you will describe the type of program you will be developing and how you will be expanding or changing.

Production Plan
The materials and labor you will need to complete your goal should be detailed in this area of the plan.

Services to Be Rendered
This should be a detailed description of the service you will be providing your customers.

Labor Requirements
How many employees you will be needing will be covered in this section. You should also include a job description summary for each employee.

Marketing Ideas
Your plan for marketing your children's theater company, both the classes and productions, should be described in this area.

Competition
A detailed analysis of your competition should be included here.

Financial Reports and Projections
Any past financial summaries and future projection sheets should be attached to your business plan.

YOUR RESOURCES

When you establish your business, you will need to develop a support system of professionals: accountants, attorneys, bankers, building inspectors, marketing specialists, insurance agents, and even a realtor. When you are developing a children's theater company you may be able to enlist the help of professionals who are parents of your potential members. Perhaps one child has a father who is a lawyer or maybe another child's parent is an insurance agent. Don't hesitate to ask for free advice. Most parents are willing to give you their expertise free of charge.

If you must hire a professional to assist you, make sure that they have some experience dealing with small businesses similar to yours. Interview them before making a financial commitment. Find out exactly what the charges will be and then keep a record of the time spent on your project. Never make assumptions when it comes to hiring professional assistance.

BOOKKEEPING

A successful business keeps accurate records that can tell you at any given time three things: how much money you owe, how much money is due you, and how much money you have. Without this information, you cannot see how your business is doing and where it is going. Keeping accurate records, especially for artistically minded people, can be the most difficult and uninteresting part of operating a business.

Financial records are, by far, the most important part of any business's bookkeeping. However, there are two other kinds of records that are vital to a children's theater operation. One is registration records on the children enrolled in your program, and the other is program books on the plays you have produced.

Keeping accurate records in all three areas will provide the data which will enable you to prove your success as a business operator.

FINANCIAL RECORDS

Financial records list all of your income and expenses. These records will be invaluable in establishing budgets for future productions and determining yearly tuition costs. They are also a necessity when filing federal, state, and local tax statements. You should keep four kinds of financial records:

1. A business checkbook which shows each check you have written on the business account. The records should include the check number, who it was written to, the amount of the check, and the reason for its use.

2. An expense ledger which lists all of the expenses you incur. This can be listed by month and by category according to the type of expense.

3. A sales journal which lists the total income per date from tuitions, productions, concessions, and other miscellaneous sales.

4. A payment due record which is a listing of all bills due, the amount of money owed, and the service rendered.

At the end of each quarter, or for smaller businesses at the end of each calendar or fiscal year, you will want to prepare a balance sheet which is a summary of the status of your business—its assets, liabilities, and net worth. The balance sheet is drawn up using the totals from your individual record accounts. It shows what you will have left when you pay all your creditors. It lists your total assets minus your liabilities, which should equal your businesses' net worth. Your accountant can help you in preparing a balance sheet which can prove invaluable in making future financial decisions.

Accurate financial records are needed to request loans or credit, prepare income tax returns, and prove your business worth.

There are a multitude of commercial financial record keeping systems available to small businesses today. In establishing your own financial record system, it is important to choose one in which you can easily keep track of and decipher your financial standing at any given time.

REGISTRATION RECORDS

When I had eleven students in my program, I kept track of their names, addresses, ages, and parents' names in a small spiral notebook. Now that I have over two hundred students, it has become a necessity to have a more accurate way of maintaining information on my Stagedoor Kids. To do this, I use a computer program and enter changes on a weekly basis.

Information I keep on my computer lists:

- Student's name
- Age and birthdate
- Address
- Home phone number
- Parent's names
- Parent's work phones
- Date the child joined the program
- Titles of plays the child has appeared in and the part played
- Class section the child attends

Registration records are invaluable when you are compiling program information for any particular play. You will have a student's history already entered in your computer and you just have to tap into it.   Registration records are also useful in determining what part in a play a child deserves. By looking back at the child's entry, you can determine if they have played a lead role or are due for one. Registration records also help you in case of emergencies when a child's parents have to be reached quickly. We also use them to list birthdays and send cards to the birthday child from Stagedoor.

PROGRAM RECORDS

As your children's theater company grows you will want to keep an accurate record of the plays your group has performed, the success of the play, and the cost factor in producing the play. I have several plays that I enjoy repeating every four or five years because they are easy to produce and popular with audiences. Recently, I re-directed *Tumbleweeds,* a western melodrama produced by Pioneer Press. When we did it originally it was a big favorite with the cast and we had a good turnout. By looking back in my records I was able to determine how much the play cost to produce. I could then examine which costs had been extravagant and where we could trim our budget for another production.

I use one ledger for my program records. I fill out one page for each play I produce (see the example on the following page).

This past year I restaged *Tumbleweeds* and the notes from my previous production helped me determine ticket price, cast the play, and establish my budget. I was also able to eliminate the musical director because in looking over my notes I remembered that the songs were quite easy to learn.

Program records can also be an asset when determining the type of plays that are popular with audiences. Over the years my program records have given me proof that the most popular plays for the family audience are fairy tales.

NAME OF PRODUCTION: Tumbleweeds

DATE OF PRODUCTION: August

PLACE: Willows Restaurant

CAST SIZE: 36

DIRECTOR: Judy Hackbarth

MUSICAL DIRECTOR: Jane Thompson

SET CONSTRUCTION: John Hackbarth

CHOREOGRAPHER: Laura Rudy

SET COSTS: $250

COSTUMES: $300

PROPS: $175

SPECIAL COSTUME NEEDS: Horse

SPECIAL PROP NEEDS: Indian hatchets, rifles, parasols

SCENERY: White & black set with wooden flats

SCRIPTS: 20 in stock

MUSICAL SCRIPT: In stock

ACCOMPANIMENT TAPE: In stock

POSTER: Logo from company, in stock

TICKET PRICE: $7 dinner, $5 brunch

LEADS: Nathan Isaac, Nina Heebink, Adam Thompson, Ben Frederick

ADVERTISING SPECIALS: None

LIGHTING: Community theater lights operated by Craig Carlson

TICKETS SOLD: 175 - dinner, 200 - brunch

SPECIAL NOTES: Dinner theater not popular with families with small children. We mostly had grandparents/parents. Popular play with the cast, easy to stage. Great songs, easy to learn!

ADVERTISING: Posters, news releases, newspaper ads three weeks before production.

Ledger for program records.

PLANNING A BUDGET

To an artistically minded creative person, the idea of planning a budget for anything can be overwhelming. Personally, I don't think in terms of facts and figures. I do not have a logical mind. I'm a person of fantasy, which is what makes me so popular with children. Unfortunately, in order to run a financially successful program, popularity with children doesn't help. I'm lucky in that I have a very logical, business minded spouse who has been able to keep me on the right track whenever I start to overspend. And, when you are running your own business, overspending is common.

When I established myself as a business, I had three types of budgets I had to establish. One was my overall business budget. This included rent on the facility, telephone, heat and electrical bills, office supplies, postage, insurance, and taxes. Another budget was for the classes I taught. This budget included supplies, advertising, and travel expenses. I also had to establish a budget for each individual production I would be staging during the year. Each budget was vital to the success of my program, and together they formed my financial guide for the year.

THE BUSINESS BUDGET

In your initial year in business you will have a variety of start-up costs in this budget. When setting up your opening budget you must estimate which costs will be first-year start-up costs and which costs will be weekly, monthly, and yearly expenses.

A typical monthly business budget for a children's theater company of 150 to 200 students might include:

Expenses	Monthly	Annual
Rent	$ 500	$ 6,000
Utilities	300	3,600
Telephone	150	1,800
Office Supplies	100	1,200
Office Postage	100	1,200
Dues & Publications	50	600
Legal & Accounting	50	600
Travel & Entertainment	50	600
Miscellaneous	200	2,400
Insurance	150	1,800
TOTAL	$1,650	$19,800

The expenses in this budget will be met with income received from your productions and classes.

THE PRODUCTION BUDGET

In putting together a children's theater production there will always be things to spend money on. Costumes, props, scenery, programs, tickets, and makeup are all realistic needs. However, the amount of money you spend in each area must be consistent with the amount of money you will be taking in from ticket sales. It sounds logical, but as you get into production for a play, logic goes out the window.

Picture yourself two days before opening and you still need several vital props, costumes, and set pieces. Naturally, you are not going to take time at that point to evaluate if you are getting the best price. You need that specific costume or that specific prop and you will pay whatever you have to pay to get it. This is where the majority of money will be wasted.

When I was directing plays for the public school system I was often frustrated and angry when my supervisors wouldn't allow me to purchase an expensive item for my set. Now that I have directors working for me, I find that I am now the one asking just how important the item is or if they can find it anywhere cheaper or substitute something else. I realize, now, that there is just so much money in the budget, and whenever we can cut corners we have to do it.

A budget needs to be established weeks before the production or classes begin, and then it needs to become a firm guide for spending. If you have estimated that you will need approximately $200 for costumes, you cannot suddenly decide to spend $500. If you do spend $500 on costumes, then you need to cut costs in other areas, but never exceed the total amount you have budgeted for a play.

Let's take a look at a typical children's play. Suppose you are staging *Tom Sawyer*. Here's a sample budget:

Cast of approximately 25

Costumes	$ 250
Props	75
Makeup	50
Set Materials	400
Royalties, 3 performances	300
Scripts	100
Tickets	50
Programs	100
Posters	25
TOTAL	$1350

This gives you a total budget of $1350 in expenses. You should also determine what percentage of your business budget must be covered in each production's cost. Next, you must figure out projected ticket sales to find out if the cost of staging this play is worthwhile to your company.

PRODUCTION BUDGET	
Ticket Income	
(No. of Seats) X (Cost of Tickets) X (No. of Performances)	
Scripts	
Royalties	
Director	
Musical Director	
Technical Director	
Costumes	
Set construction Materials	
Props	
Makeup	
Lighting/Sound Technician	
Posters	
Tickets	
Newspaper Advertising	
Total Production Costs	
Net Income	

Suppose you have a theater with a seating capacity of two hundred and are charging a ticket price of $5. If you perform the play three times, that gives you a total of $3000, if you sell out every performance. Assuming you have no other expenses, this would be a profitable play for your group to perform. If, however, you are paying rent on the theater, and hiring a musical director, a light technician, and, possibly even a technical director; your expenses will rapidly outscale your budget. You would need to adjust your ticket price to meet your budget needs.

In figuring out the actual budget I would never assume all performances will be sellouts. I figure my budgets at 50 percent of total seating capacity so that I am assured I will make a profit from each production.

The chart on the opposite page can help you figure out your production budget for an individual play. Use it as your guide to establish a firm budget and you will have a financially successful play.

THE CLASS BUDGET

Income from the acting classes will be used to cover expenses accrued in both the business budget and losses incurred in productions. But, you will also have expenses in the classes that will have to be budgeted. Perhaps you need art supplies or costumes or copies of a skit. Expenses in the classes should be minimal unless you are paying teachers. A sample monthly class budget for ten acting classes of fifteen students each might involve:

paper	$ 25
teacher resource materials	25
costumes and props	25
miscellaneous	50
Total	$125

When deciding on your tuition fee, you should estimate both your class budget and your business budget, and then set tuitions accordingly.

INSURANCE

One of the hardest realities I had to face when establishing my own children's theater company was that a good part of my income would go into paying for insurance. When I had worked for the public school system and for the community education program, I never had to worry about insurance. The school administration took care of it. When I became an independent business person liable for the safety of the children in my program, insurance suddenly became a necessity.

Children are just naturally accident prone. No matter how many times you tell them NOT to jump from the stage, there is always one child who thinks he or she is invincible. Insurance is for that child!

Whether you own or rent a facility, insurance will safeguard your business against losses from fire, illness, and injury. You cannot operate without it.

FINDING THE RIGHT INSURANCE COMPANY

Selecting an insurance company can be a challenge for anyone. When you have an unusual business to insure, it becomes even more of a challenge. When I first approached my personal insurance agent for coverage on my business, he was somewhat perplexed as to what category we came under. At the time, I did not own my own building so I only needed coverage for the classes I was teaching and the plays I produced. There was no category specifically aimed at my type of business. Finally, the insurance company decided I came under the same heading as dance school, and we were able to establish some rates.

Although the insurance agent I approached for business coverage had insured my home for several years, I still felt I needed several different quotes before selecting business insurance. By placing my original agent into a bidding race for my business coverage, I was able to obtain the best possible rates; several hundred dollars below what he originally quoted me.

In addition to evaluating a company for the best rates, you will also want to take into consideration the financial stability of the insurance company you are interviewing. You may get a lower rate from a lesser known insurance agency, but will it still be in business the next year? The reputation of a company can be just as important as the coverage you will be receiving. You need a guarantee that you will receive the coverage should you need it.

When you meet with an individual representative from an insurance agency, do a walk-through inspection with the agent. If you have a facility in which you will consistently hold classes or productions, meet the agent there and show him exactly what you will be doing. Get a list of specific exclusions that the policy will not cover, and ask for an explanation as to why not. Find out how much you can save in a deductible package. What is the difference between a one hundred dollar deductible and a five hundred dollar deductible.

Ask as many questions as you can before selecting the right agency. Don't hesitate to let a variety of companies know you are bidding out your business insurance looking for the lowest price available. Take your time and select the best insurance package you can find.

KINDS OF INSURANCE COVERAGE

Basically you will need three kinds of insurance:

- Liability for injuries in your acting classes.
- Liability for the audiences who attend your performances.
- Liability for any products you may sell at your productions.

In addition you may need:

- Property insurance, if you own or rent your own facility.
- Workman's compensation, if you have any employees or volunteer labor.

Optional insurances you may want to obtain are:

- Disability income protection in case you become disabled.
- Business interruption insurance in case your facility is damaged by fire or some other cause.
- Business life insurance which can provide funds for transition in case you die.

Before you sign the final papers for insurance coverage be sure you read and understand all of the fine print in the policy. It is a good idea to reevaluate business insurance needs about every six months.

A DREAM BECOMES A BUSINESS

Nine years into teaching my own drama classes I made a decision. I needed my own building! The number of students in my program had grown to well over one hundred and it was getting more and more difficult to hold classes at the Catholic school. In order to meet all my students' needs, I needed to teach more than one day a week, and that made scheduling additional class time a problem. As the numbers grew in the classes, so did the number of plays I directed. Up to that point I had been directing two majors plays a year, one in the summer and one at Christmas time. At those times of the year it was relatively easy to reserve performing spaces. When I began to add productions I consistently ran into difficulties finding places to stage our plays.

The stress of juggling times and places was becoming overwhelming. I decided the time had come to either find a building for my Stagedoor program or choose a different line of work. I decided to search for six months and if no permanent space looked promising, I would phase out my program.

My husband and I tried several different options before discovering our present location. We drew up our own plans for a theater/classroom facility. The construction quotes were, of course,

Some of the students enrolled in the Stagedoor program.

outrageous. We looked into renting space. Few places could meet our safety requirements. And then the Gem Theater came up for sale.

The Gem had been New Richmond's movie theater for several decades. It was a decaying, disgusting building that only the most desperate of movie goers dared enter anymore. It had been built around 1917 by W.S. Shannon. In 1927 it was purchased by Jack and Carrie Heywood, who established it as one of the first movie theaters in the area, bringing the wonder of the silent cinema to surrounding citizens. The first talkies were shown there in 1931.

Throughout the years the Gem had undergone various changes and renovations. Somewhere around the early 1930s, possibly when the Heywood's first obtained the building, beautiful art-deco murals were painted along the theater's interior. Several years later when the echo of the movie's sound system reverberated off the walls, these beautiful murals were hidden away behind heavy gold curtains. Cinemascope arrived in the 1950s and more remodeling was done, including enlarging the screen and installing a terrazzo floor in the lobby. The Heywoods did everything they could to assure that the Gem was the most elite movie theater in the area.

In the summer of 1960 the Gem made history, not with a movie but with a live appearance by the country's future president, John F. Kennedy, who addressed potential voters from the Gem's stage. However, after President Kennedy's appearance, the Gem began to decline. As the Heywood's grew older, they tried a variety of different managers, but no one had their enthusiasm for the theater and gradually deterioration set in. In the fall of 1990, the Gem closed with little fanfare. Like many movie theaters, it had fallen victim to the high cost of booking films and the constant competition from home videos.

We purchased the Gem building in November of 1990; and thus, the Stagedoor Players Performing Arts Center was born.

When I announced to the Stagedoor Kids that we had purchased the Gem theater for our new Stagedoor home, they were not impressed. Everyone in town was familiar with the state of the Gem and few believed it could ever be remodeled successfully. Fortunately, whether they believed it or not, the parents and kids decided to back us and even offered to help. Over 150 volunteers, young and old, joined us in applying buckets of paint and elbow grease to help renovate the vintage building. Kids as little as five-years old helped us scrape old gum off of seats, rip out walls, haul in tons of insulation, and participated in all the other disgusting jobs involved in a major remodeling project. And the parents showed up too! Almost every weekend during the remodeling, we would average between 25 to 40 people working on turning our theater into the Stagedoor home.

The project became a mixture of emotions. It was a nightmare of long days and even nights of hard work. At the same time it created an incredible feeling of togetherness and pride among all the Stagedoor families who worked on turning the old Gem into a Performing Arts Center.

Early on in the remodeling process we decided to recreate as much of the original 1930s atmosphere as possible. We wanted to create a facility that gave audiences a step back in time to the days when theater presentations were truly a family event. We couldn't be happier about the results.

Entering the lobby area today, audiences can imagine themselves in the days of silent movies and vaudeville. The original ticket booth greets customers along with an antique costume display and beautifully restored art-deco murals that line the walls of the theater itself. While the lower lobby offers a theater memorabilia room for local history buffs, a gift store called the Prop Shop on the main level provides theater goers with colorful souvenirs. All in all, it is a place people want to experience.

A performance in the Stagedoor Players Performing Arts Center.

Owning your own theater is a dream few directors can ever hope to achieve. When I started teaching and directing drama over ten years ago, owning my own building wasn't even in my thoughts. Today, Stagedoor Center is one of the busiest places in town. It is the place the Stagedoor Kids hang out whether they have a class or not. After school or on weekends, the kids will often just drop by to watch a rehearsal or wait until their parents finish work. They feel comfortable being in our building because they know they are an important part of it. Occasionally, we now stage adult performances, but our overall objective has been met as we continue to remain a for-profit children's theater.

RESOURCES

COMPANIES

The following companies produce an assortment of scripts for children's plays as well as books on theater and the performing arts. Send them a 9 x 12-inch, self-addressed envelop with three first class stamps and ask them for copies of their catalogs.

I. E. Clark, Inc.
P.O. Box 246
Schulenburg, TX 78956

Clarus Music, Ltd.
340 Bellevue Avenue
Yonkers, NY 10703

Contemporary Drama Service
P.O. Box 7710
Colorado Springs, CO 80933

Dramatic Publishing Company
311 Washington Street
Woodstock, IL 60098

Samuel French, Inc.
45 W. 25th Street
New York, NY 10010

Pioneer Drama Service
P.O. Box 22555
Denver, CO 80222

Players Press, Inc.
P.O. Box 1132
Studio City, CA 91604

BOOKS

The following books will be useful for further reference for beginning a theater company or teaching classes in children's drama. Together they would make an excellent children's theater library.

Act It Out! by Lynn Molyneux; Trellis Books, 1985. Quick and easy skits to use with children's drama groups.

Amazing Alligators by Mazine Riggers; Monday Morning Press, 1990. A variety of ideas for working with the youngest children. Activities are given for art, music, and creative dramatics.

Clown Act Omnibus by Wes McVicar; Meriwether Publishing Co., 1987. This clown guidebook offers some interesting pantomime and improvisation exercises that are sure to delight children.

Creative Clowning by Bruce Fife, et. al.; Piccadilly Books, 1992. An excellent text on clowning and comedy techniques.

Curtain I by Susan Thomas and Susan Dinges; Trillium Press, 1986. Creative dramatic activities for elementary children.

Curtain II by Susan Thomas and Susan Dinges; Trillium Press, 1986. More creative dramatic activities for elementary children.

The Drama & Theatre Arts Course Book by David Self; Players Press, 1994. A practical handbook for teaching advanced dramatic arts. Also contains a history of theatre.

Encore! More Winning Monologues for Young Actors by Peg Kehret; Meriwether Publishing Co., 1988. A good selection of monologues for young people.

Hey Gang Let's Put On a Show by Linda Williams Aber; Instructor Books, 1987. A compilation of skits, poems, and plays for child actors.

Improvisation for the Theatre by Viola Spolin; Northwestern University Press, 1983. A valuable guide for improvisation exercises.

Incredible Indoor Games Book by Bob Gregson; Fearon Teacher Aids, 1982. A good resource guide for group cohesion ideas, movement, and concentration skill builders.

Instructor's Big Book of Plays; Instructor Publications, 1983. An elementary educator's handbook for the language arts which contains many practical ideas for developing creative dramatic skills in young children.

The Language Arts Idea Book by Joanne Schaff; Goodyear Publishing Co., 1976. An elementary educator's handbook for the language arts which contains many practical ideas for developing creative dramatic skills in young children.

Look, Listen and Trust by George Rawlins and Jillian Rich; Players Press, 1992. An outstanding book of games and activities to increase confidence on and off stage.

Kids in Motion by Julie Weissman; Alfred Publishing Co., 1986. This book and accompanying tape offers complete exercises for warm-up and movement.

Mime Time by Happy Jack Feder. Meriwether Publishing Co., 1992. Funny, fast mime skits guaranteed to thrill young drama students.

More Short Plays for the Classroom by Juanita Bryson; Educational Insights, 1982. The short plays in this publication can be valuable in beginning dialogue development.

The Moving Center by Gay and Kathlyn Hendricks; Prentice-Hall, 1983. A great guide for beginning movement activities.

Overhead Transparencies for Creative Drama; Creative Teaching Press, 1989. A colorful collection of transparencies and short narrative stories to use in building improvisational skills.

Pantomimes 101 by James W. Gousseff; Art Craft Play Co., 1974. This book contains valuable pantomimes to use with the individual performer or with small groups. The difficulty ranges from beginning drama students to the more advanced thespians.

Plays Children Love edited by Coleman A. Jennings and Aurand Harris; Doubleday & Co., 1981. Probably the most valuable collection of popular children's plays.

Playing the Game by Christine Poultey; Players Press, 1991. The best performing arts game book available, easy to use.

Putting On a Play by Susan and Stephan Judy; Charles Scribner's Sons, 1982. An extensive collection of beginning drama activities including an abundance of improvisation and pantomime exercises.

Secrets and Surprises by Joe Wayman; Good Apple Press, 1977. Detailed activities for building skills in pantomime, group cohesion, and improvisational skills.

Singing Games and Play Party Games compiled by Richard Chase; Dover Publications, 1949. An excellent book for movement and group cohesion activities. There are detailed descriptions for a variety of folk dances which are sure to enhance any children's group.

Speech Activities in the High School by William Z. Buys; National Textbook Co., 1967. An older resource guide that contains some solid dialogue exercises.

Stage Make-up Techniques by Martin Jans; Players Press Inc., 1992. Covers the basic techniques of stage makeup as well as gives detailed examples of a variety of stage characters. Very applicable to children's theater.

Stage Management and Theatre Administration by Pauline Menear and Terry Hawkins; Schirmer Books, 1989. A great guide for the beginning theater administrator. Contains how-tos on a variety of management questions including setting up budgets, hiring staff, and finding facilities.

Strutter's Complete Guide to Clown Makeup by Jim Roberts; Piccadilly Books, 1991. A step-by-step guide on designing and applying clown makeup. Used by professional clowns.

Theater Games by Viola Spolin; Northwestern University Press, 1985. Many of the activities detailed in this book may be too difficult for younger children, but it is a good guide to keep on hand when working with the more advanced theater group.

Theatre Games for Young Performers by Marian C. Novelly; Meriwether Publishing Co., 1985. A multitude of theater activities for older children. Many of the ideas in this book can be adapted for younger children.

The Young Actor's Workbook by Judith Roberts Seto; Grove Press Inc., 1984. Activities are geared more towards the older adolescent. Some valuable dialogue exercises.

INDEX